I0558644

THE

DIVINE
WAY TO HELP

CHISTIANS
IN

TROUBLED TIMES

THE

DIVINE
WAY TO HELP

CHISTIANS
IN

TROUBLED TIMES

DR. BROU ATCHE

ARPress
ILLUMINATING IDEAS
EMPOWERING VOICES

The publication contains the opinions and ideas of the author, who intends to offer information of the general nature. Any reliance on the information herein contained is at the reader's own discretion.

The author and printer specifically disclaim all responsibility for any liability, loss, or right, personal or otherwise, which is incurred as a consequence, directly, of the use and application of any contents of the book. They further make no warranties or representations with respect to any implied warranty of fitness for a particular purpose. Any recommendation are made without any guarantee on the part of the author or printer.

ARPress
45 Dan Road Suite 36
Canton MA 02021

Hotline: 1(888) 821-0229
Fax: 1(508) 545-7580

Ordering Information:
Quantity Sales. Special discounts are available on quantity purchases by corporations, associations, and others. For details, contact the publisher at the address above.

All the Scripture quotations, unless otherwise, are taken from the King James Bible (KJB), 1979 edition.

Printed in the United States of America.

ISBN-13   Paperback   979-8-89389-234-5
               eBook   979-8-89389-235-2

Library of Congress Control Number: 2024906334

ABSTRACT

Our work focuses on God's way to help Christians in troubled times with the intention of establishing differences between therapeutic approaches to counselling. Christians who come to Canada for a long stay or to settle there like any immigrant face many changes in their lives including divorce or separation, psychosomatic illnesses and anxiety disorders, conjugal violence, recurrent unemployment, etc. All this can be attributed to poor adaptation or difficult acculturation leading to a gradual abandonment of the Christian faith.

The challenges are so great that the most weak are moving away from God's face to transgress His laws. What therapeutic approach should be used to help them restore faith in God? Several pastors have integrated psychology into theology from a therapeutic perspective, but the results have been ineffective. Biblical and psychological counselling cannot be combined. The main objective of our work is to show that the biblical approach to the counselling helps to restore the trust in relationship and bring the sinner back to God.

In this work, it was necessary for us to meet with other pastors to get information about their practice in counselling. The particularity of our work has greatly affected the Christian immigrant community, whose needs are increasingly great. Several problematic cases have been followed up in biblical counselling. Thus, in each case, we have: (1) accompanied a person possessed by a spirit to regain tripartite balance (mind, body and soul), (2) provided assistance to someone seeking marriage, (3) followed a person struggling with a divorce problem, (4) helped a couple with a problem of adultery and infertility, (5) accompanied a couple in conflict with idolatry, infidelity and immorality, (6) analyzed the painful experience of an inconsolable and depressive woman.

The case study made it possible to analyse each situation in depth in its context and to conclude that, unlike the psychotherapeutic approach, biblical counselling remains unequivocally the path of excellence to restore the balance of the tripartite components "body, mind and soul" and to make peace with God.

Keywords : God's way, Christians, psychotherapeutic approach, biblical counselling, immigrant Christians

DEDICATION OF THE BOOK

"And the LORD said unto Moses, They shall offer their offering, each prince on his day, for the dedicating of the altar." (*Nu. 7:11*)

I dedicate this work

To Leocadie my wife, the love of my life for her indescribable and undeniable psychological, practical and material support and who has accepted so much my several hours spent in libraries and my various study tours. May God continue to bless you and make his face shine upon you. May he command health and peace to be with you always.

" *Song for the dedication of the house. From David.* I will extol thee, O LORD; for thou hast lifted me up, and hast not made my foes to rejoice over me." (*Ps. 30:1*)

I dedicate this work

To my deceased father Atche Gilbert for his love and his financial support in my childhood. I dedicace also this book to my deceased mother N'Guessan Marcelline Kakou for the unique and crucial role she played in my life as a child. (Jb. 1:21)

" And the children of Israel, the priests, and the Levites, and the rest of the children of the captivity, kept the dedication of this house of God with joy " (Ezr. 6:16).

I dedicate this thesis

To all my children: Christian Brou, Gilbert Norio-Stéphane, Gerard N'Guessan, Alexandre Jean-Simon, Marie-Elisabeth and Emmanuel-Yeshua Brou, for their patience and collaboration during my studies. Daddy loves you.

FOREWORD

Give thanks in all circumstances; for this is God's
will for you in Christ Jesus. (1 Th. 5:18)

This work is the result of several years of work and reflection
on the practice of biblical counselling. The theological
approach applied in this work combines both methodical
field research and personal reflection on biblical counselling.
It is also the result of a professional and personal experience.
This work does not pretend in any way to have answered
all the questions or to have rebuilt biblical counselling, but
I hope that its content can be used by God's servants to
encourage people in counselling situations to study the Bible,
to want to meet God, to follow a clear direction towards
specific changes. Several people have given me considerable
help in its accomplishment and, in several aspects, this work
is based on teamwork involving experienced pastors and
qualified people.

First of all, I would like to thank, Dr. Jenkins Terrance
(Ph. D.), founder of the Montreal School of Ministry
(M. S. O. M.) and member of the Evangelical Order of
Certified Pastoral Counsellors of America, who advised me
throughout this work and whose comments increased my
confidence and courage during particularly difficult stages.
Dr. Jenkins Terrance has revived my interest in studying
practical theology. His rigour in terms of Christian doctrine
and his reflections has always aroused my admiration. I

would also like to thank all my predecessors, Dr. Mulopo Nzam Bakombo, (Ph. D.) President of Fondation Sauver la Famille, Dr. Bernard Dufour, who advised me and provided me with spiritual support throughout this work. I would also like to thank Dr. Stephen Hambly (Ph. D.) for giving me this opportunity to present this work.

Special thanks to Reverend André Quesnel, coordinator and Reverend Ted McLean, president of the Global Christian Ministry Forum Canada. Finally, I would like to thank all the graduating students of my Bible school (Christian Institute of Biblical Ministry), who through their interest in the online Bible course, recognized my counselling skills and trusted me.

The collaboration with the church Centre Evangélique La Rédemption Divine (C. E. R. D.) which I founded as a pastor, allowed me to carry out pastoral practice and especially to meet people whose stories inspired me in some of the case illustrations. I would have hardly succeeded without the prayers of the members of my church.

TABLE OF CONTENTS

CHAPTER III: COUNSELLING THROUGHOUT BIBLICAL TIME

CHAPTER IV: THE HUMAN BEING, ITS TRIPARTITE NATURE AND DISEASES

CHAPITER VI: DISCUSSION AND PERSONNAL VIEWPOINT

ABBREVIATIONS AND ACRONYMS

Old Testament

Gn.	Genesis
Ex.	Exodus
Lv.	Leviticus
Nu.	Numbers
Dt.	Deuteronomy
Jsh.	Joshua
Jg.	Judges
Ru.	Ruth
1Sa.	1 Samuel
2Sa.	2 Samuel
1Ki.	1 Kings
2Ki.	2 Kings
1Ch.	1 Chronicles
2Ch.	2 Chronicles
Ezr.	Ezra
Ne.	Nehemiah
Es	Esther
Jb.	Job
Ps.	Psalms
Pr.	Proverbs
Ec.	Ecclesiastes
Cant.	Song of Solomon
Is.	Isaiah
Jr.	Jeremiah
La.	Lamentations
Eze.	Ezekiel
Da.	Daniel

Ho.	Hosea
Jl.	Joel
Am.	Amos
Ob.	Obadiah
Jon.	Jonah
Mi.	Micah
Na.	Nahum
Hb.	Habakkuk
Zp.	Zephaniah
Hg.	Haggai
Zec.	Zechariah
Ml.	Malachi

New Testament

Mt.	Matthew
Mk.	Mark
Lk.	Luke
Jn.	John
Ac.	Acts of the Apostles
Ro.	Romans
Co.	Corinthians
Ga.	Galatians
Eph.	Ephesians
Phil.	Philippians
Col.	Colossians
1 Th.	1 Thessalonians
2 Th.	2 Thessalonians
1 Tim.	1 Timothy
2 Tim.	2 Timothy
Ti.	Titus
Phm.	Philemon
Heb.	Hebrews
Jm.	James
1P.	1 Peter
2P.	2 Peter
1 Jn.	1 John
2 Jn.	2 John
3 Jn.	3 John

| Jd. | Jude |
| Re. | Revelation |

INTRODUCTION

Biblical counselling is one of the most important ministerial tools that God established within his people, the Word of God[1] declares:

> *"Now therefore come, let me, I pray thee, give thee counsel, that thou mayest save thine own life, and the life of thy son Solomon."*

The Bible shows that the people of God can die due to the lack of advice. The Christian counselor can thus help those who suffer and who look sincerely for the divine assistant. The counselling ministry is vital for the health, the balance and the sustainability of the Church. Nowadays, the biblical counselling is neglected in the body of Christ. One of the main causes of this negligence is due to the factors of lack of vocation, lack of time of the ministers, and the fault of knowledge of the Word of God.

Many ministers went as far as recommending their believers to non-Christian psychologists and psychiatrists, for reasons of incompetence regarding counselling while they should take care of it in the Church. In addition, the emergence of psychotherapies strongly influences Christian counselling[2], so today we are seeing ambiguous and controversial approaches

---

[1] 1 Kings 1: 12, KJV

[2] Jenkins Terrance, *Christian Counselling: Godly Principles to Help You in Time of Need*. Baltimore, Publish America, 2009, p.9.

to counselling in the church. As a result, counselling in God's church is declining.

Furthermore, Christian counselling was influenced by various currents and thoughts such as the Freudian theory (psychoanalyses) and Rogerian Therapy (Person–Centered Therapy), as if the Bible was not sufficient to bring answers to the suffering of the people. Indeed, the various theories above mentioned are in complete opposition to the biblical revelation. In contrast, in the approach of Jay Adams (Nouthetic counselling), he does not consider psychotherapy, because he considers in his approach that counselling is an exhortation by means of adequate biblical verses. Jay Adams supports the fact that any counselling is fundamentally theological[3].

Besides, the current situation in the field of counselling requires unequivocally a return to the biblical foundations. The purpose of the biblical counselling is to bring real change to the personality of the person advised to allow him to walk according to the biblical standard. It is advisable to note that this type of counselling is lavished on the people who are convinced that God is able by the power of His Holy Spirit to effect changes in their life. This type of spiritual support concerns at first the human interiority and its relational consequences.

The counselee must agree to be confronted and guided by the Word of God. The apostle Paul[4] mentions that:

> "All Scripture is given by inspiration of God, and is profitable for doctrine, for reproof, for correction, for instruction in righteousness, that

---

[3] Paul MILLEMAN, *La relation d'aide, vocation de l'Église*, France, Éditions Excelsis, 2014. 480 p.

[4] 2 Timothy 3. 16-17, KJV

the man of God may be complete, thoroughly equipped for every good work."

It is generally accepted that biblical counseling is done for the benefit of a person in trouble with a broken heart. The opening statement of the ministry of the Lord tells us in these words[5]:

> "The Spirit of the Lord is upon me, because he hath anointed me to preach the gospel to the poor; he hath sent me to heal the brokenhearted, to preach deliverance to the captives, and recovering of sight to the blind, to set at liberty them that are bruised, to preach the acceptable year of the Lord."

This passage teaches us the importance of the ministerial mission of Jesus and contains the purpose of counselling emanating from the Spirit of God. In biblical counselling, faith in Jesus and adherence to the Word of God are determining and necessary factors in the therapy of the suffering person. It should be noted that in the canonical gospels, the evangelists reported many conversations of Jesus with suffering people in search of healing, restoration or consolation: this is the case of the Canaanite woman who begged Jesus to have mercy of her daughter possessed by a devil. At the sight of her great faith in Jesus, her daughter was healed (Mt. 15: 21-28).

The same is true of Jesus' encounter with the rich and influential young man who had a false perception of the true nature of salvation (Mk. 10: 17-27). It is also the case of the encounter of Jesus with Zacchaeus, the publican, the lost, who was saved by receiving Jesus in his house (Lk. 19:1-10). The example of the marginal Samaritan woman who receives salvation following an interview with Jesus can also convince

---

[5] Luke 4. 18-19, KJV

us of it (Jn. 4:7-42). All these deliverances and healings were possible through the faith of suffering people and power in the Word of Jesus Christ.

This work is intended as a reference tool for Christians seeking biblical counselling. Behind the term, "counselling" there are multiple approaches. Counselling is part of a framework that determines its spirit and biblical context. By frame, we mean a set of factors including the biblical approach, the socio-cultural determinants of therapy, and some fixed parameters such as frequency of sessions, time limit, use of the Word of God, and faith in Jesus Christ.

What interests us in this work is, first, to list the different approaches in counselling and, second, to specify what these differences favor in the therapeutic process. We are going to group the main non-biblical psychotherapies approaches to counselling under the cover four currents: psychoanalytic approach; behavioral and cognitive approach and systemic approach; as well as psychotherapies, according to the humanist prospect.

Our work will have six chapters. In the first chapter, we will try to define the concept of counselling and its objective, as well as its contribution to the therapy of the suffering person. In the second chapter, we will compare secular counselling and counselling from a biblical perspective. To do this, we will discuss some aspects of the biblical counselling. The third chapter will be devoted to counselling through Biblical times without forgetting to highlight the work of the Holy Spirit, the Comforter. It will then be possible for us to see how the advice was practiced in Jesus' time. The fourth chapter will focus on the human being, his tripartite nature and his health problems. The fifth chapter will deal with immigrant Christians and biblical counselling. To do this, we will discuss some examples of case studies. Finally, in Chapter

Six, we will return to the elements of the biblical counselling that seemed most important to us and which raised questions in us or led us to further reflection. Finally, a brief conclusion will conclude this work.

CHAPTER I

THE COUNSELLING

1. 1. Definition

The psychology of counselling today has a vitality and growth that is both exciting for its counselors and beneficial for the community in general. Many people are looking for someone to listen to their problem, get help, and at the same time ask for an answer that reflects the complexity of the environmental problems surrounding their problems.

Counselling is a wide and complex concept that requires a lot of attention in its understanding and use. This concept of counselling implies the existence of a unilateral link of assistance between two or more persons. It is present in several areas and its definition depends on the context in which it is applied.

The word "counselling" can have multiple meanings, such as offering advice and encouragement, sharing wisdom and skills, setting goals and resolving conflicts. Counsellors often search the past for repairing the present. Sometimes they explore the possible effects of physical and chemical imbalances that can cause physiological problems. An important part of the counselling resolves and restores conflicts between people.

The specific purpose of any counselling is undoubtedly accompanying suffering with the help of a resource person. It is based on the classic schema: questioning, understanding, interpretation, support and evaluation. In all counselling, the quality of active counselling plays a decisive role in communication.

On the other hand, the American psychologist Carl Rogers has developed an approach centered on the individual. According to C. Rogers, counselling is the whole relationship of at least one of the two protagonists seeking to foster in the other growth, development, maturity, better functioning and a high capacity to face life[6].

In addition, C. Rogers argues that the individual has considerable resources in himself to understand himself, to perceive himself differently, to change his fundamental attitudes and behavior towards himself. But only a clearly definable climate, made up of psychological attitudes facilitating, can enable him to access his resources[7]. Other authors embarked on the same theory.

Claude Buchhold (1984) argues that counselling touches interiority, that is, heart, soul, and thought[8]. Several principles therefore seem to become clear from these different conceptions and definitions of the counselling.

Patton (1976) summarizes on this subject a personal synthesis which is expressed in this way[9]:

---

[6] C. ROGERS, *Le développement de la personne*, Paris, Dunod-InterÉdition, 2005, p. 27.

[7] Carl ROGERS, Les caractéristiques d'une approche centrée sur la personne. http://www.acp-pr.org/caracteristiques.html. Consulted on 2017-04-30.

[8] William KIRWAN, *Biblical Concepts for Christian Counselling, A case for Integrating Psychology and Theology*, Baker Book House Company (Grand Rapids), 1984.p.8.

[9] Angelo BRUSCO, *Counselling pastoral et counselling psychologique (in french)* Master thesis, ULaval, 1993, p.25.

"In the light of Christian theology, pastoral counselling can be understood as the discovery of personal meaning through relational humanity, the standard of which is established by the humanity of God for and with us in Jesus Christ."

Moreover, it is important to note that there are a variety of theories that range from the simplest to the most complex.

1. 2. Who is a Counsellor

Terrance Jenkins, in his work "Christian counselling: Godly principles to help you in time of need" explains who a counsellor is. A counsellor is one who gives counsel or advises (Pr. 11:4). In the Old Testament, the counsellor most often referred to the king's advisor (2 Sa. 15:12; 1 Chr. 27:33), or one of the chief men of the government (Jb 3:14; Is. 1:26). In Mark 15 verse 43 and Luke 23 verse 50 the word "counsel" designated a "council member" of Sanhedrin, in the Gospel of John (Jn. 14:16, 26; 15:26; 16:7).

Webster's Dictionary says that to counsel is to give advice or recommend a course of action. Thus, a counsellor is one who gives advice on a course of action. Such would be a lawyer, psychologist, psychiatrist, or a Christian Counselor. The new Concise Bible Dictionary says that a counselor is one who gives advice, use of the Messiah in Isaiah 9 verse 6:

> *"For unto us a child is born, unto us a son is given: and the government shall be upon his shoulder: and his name shall be called Wonderful, Counsellor, The mighty God, The everlasting Father, The Prince of Peace."*

The Greek word has entered Christian thought as *"paraclete"* and it means one who is called to stand by someone, especially in a law-court, hence the translation as *"advocate"*. The help of the Spirit is seen in such legal terms in Matthew 10 verse 19, where the Christian is envisaged as being on trial before secular and/or Jewish authorities."

The actual Greek work *"helein"* means talk things over to plan or decide something; to seek an opinion from; to ask advice of, to refer to, or turn to, especially for information; to keep in mind while acting or deciding to show regard for. Jenkins Terrance (2009) argues that all true counselling points the counsellee to the great Counsellor, the Lord Jesus Christ. Christian counselling is not Christian counselling because it is called such. It is Christian counselling because it is counselling that has as its aim the changing of the heart of the person in relation to his Lord, and thereby changing that person's conduct and behavior.

A counsellor that is truly Christian will not use the theories of Carl Jung, Mowrer, Carl Roger or Freud, as the basis for his counselling. Rather, he will use the Word of God as his rule and the basis for his counselling and the Holy Spirit as his guide to bring about the necessary change in the person's thinking and ultimately his life.

It has been established that secular counselling focuses on the problem and the client. Christian counselling is grounded in the Bible. It helps a person embrace pain through his or her relationship with Jesus. The processes of counselling are the same, but the motivation is different. Dr. Jenkins often hears how badly a person behaved in a situation, but he seldom hears the reason for such behavior. The Bible says in Proverbs 23 verse 7:

> *"For as he thinketh in his heart, so is he: eat and drink, saith he to thee; but his heart is not with thee."*

Thus, when someone's thinking is in a negative mode, that person will act the way that he thinks. Again, people do not think badly because they feel bad, they feel bad because they think badly. A counselee's behavior does not determine his thinking, his thinking determines his behavior. Feelings do not determine one's actions; one's actions determine one's feelings. The counsellor must get to the root of the problem before he can adequately help a counsellee. One may think that behavior is the problem but that is not the case. Behavior is just a symptom of the problem within.

Psychologists and psychiatrists would like to shift the blame for a person's behavior to someone or something else. The environment in which someone grew up is considered the cause of that one drinking alcohol or using drugs. The Christian Counsellor must understand that the root of the problem is sin, not the environment or some other such thing. Thus, the Christian Counsellor must make the counselee become aware of the sin problem, and that he must take responsibility for his own behavior, and then point him to one who can change his life, Jesus Christ.

1. 3. Psychotherapies and Christian counselling

Our study here deals only with some of the main approaches to psychotherapy, as well as the perception of a biblical perspective.

1. 3.1. Different approaches in secular counselling

The concept of psychotherapy emerges in the world of biblical counselling. Psychotherapy is a discipline of the human sciences. It is a non-biblical approach to support and accompaniment. Indeed, it is a technique of care that is addressed to the people suffering from emotional problems. In general, it seeks to unmask errors in the individual's lifestyle and make him aware of the mistaken appreciation of his value in relation to a social standard. Unlike biblical counselling, whose benchmark is the Bible's lifestyle.

The practice of psychotherapy multiplied during the last decades and we count at present 400 forms of psychotherapies listed (Venisse, 2009[10]). These studies on the discipline show that it is not easy to define criteria for classifying these psychotherapies.

In addition, there is no universal standard which is recognized by psychotherapy[11]. After decades in which psychoanalysis, its heterodox derivatives, and offspring, occupied practically the whole field of psychotherapy, today we are witnessing a proliferation and a diversification of techniques. There are certainly important issues (economics, politics and alternative medicine), but the risks are not only a reality but also considerable for the Church of Jesus Christ (sectarianism, heresy, decline of religious beliefs).

In our research, we will focus on four therapeutic streams that tend to infiltrate into the Christian counselling, including Freudian psychoanalytic therapy; Behavioral and cognitive psychotherapies; Systemic therapies; and humanistic therapies.

1. 3. 1. 1. Psychoanalytic Approach

Psychoanalysis is a set of theories that explains human behavior through the dynamic influence of the unconscious. Sigmund Freud is the founding father[12]. Psychoanalytic therapies are

---

[10] Alain DENEUX, François-Xavier POUDAT, Thierry SERVILLAT, Jean-Luc VENISSE, Les psychothérapies: approche plurielle, Masson, 2009.

[11] Élise BOUDREAULT, Le cadre thérapeutique selon diverses approches en psychothérapie, (Master thesis), ULaval, 1998, p.102.

[12] Sigmund Freud was an Austrian neurologist, the father of

inspired by the theories of Sigmund Freud. These are therapies that deal with unconsciousness and the formation of personality. They focus on the relationships, events, conflicts and injuries of the past.

They consider that the psyche of the human being works based on the conflicts bound to the development of the person. The psychoanalytical therapies consider hidden strengths, that is strengths unconscious of the individual. Indeed, the psychoanalytic cure was developed by Freud from the application of the principles of hypnosis and suggestion. It is thanks to hypnosis that Freud seeks to find in his patients the memory of the traumatic factors of the past. This practice was abandoned by Freud (after 1896) to emphasize the science of dreams.

From the simple listening of the spontaneous associations, Freud will endeavor to reconstruct the past, while overcoming the resistance that obstructs access to the awareness of pathogenic situations. Thus, the famous Freudian fundamental rule emerges in these words: the patient must defend himself to let his consciousness acquire more and more precise contents of his unconscious psychic activity, he is invited to verbalize the images, the ideas, and sensations as they appear in the field of consciousness, without exercising control. According to this fundamental rule, all thought must be communicated immediately as soon as it occurs[13]. The transfer of the representations of the patient on the person

psychoanalysis. He laid the foundations of psychoanalysis and subsequently became interested in slips and missed acts to conceptualize the notion of the psychic apparatus in three parts: the conscious, the preconscious, and the unconscious. (Paul MILLEMAN, *La relation d'aide, vocation de l'Église, France, Éditions Excelsis*, 2014. p.177)

[13] Jean BERGERET, *La cure psychanalytique sur divan: les grandes découvertes sur la psychanalyse*, Tchou, 1980, p. 9-19.

of the therapist is the most valuable tool in his interpretation work but also provides elements of resistance to healing. A set of affective interactions can cause the analyst to establish counter-transference. Since Freud, psychoanalytic therapies have been enriched by the clinical and technical theories of many analysts among which some operate in the counselling. The psychoanalysis allows the patient to understand better these conflicts, to give them a new sense and to prevent them from repeating in the current life in the form of psychic symptoms. Unfortunately, this approach is incompatible with the biblical thought.

1. 3. 1. 2. Behavioral and Cognitive Psychotherapy

The behavioral and cognitive psychotherapies represent the application of psychology to psychotherapy. They put the accent on the application of an experimental approach to understand and modify the psychopathologies, which disrupt the life of a patient. This form of counselling focuses the attention on the behavior and the thoughts. The behavioral therapy acts directly on the behavior which[14] raises problem, while the cognitive therapy will take care of thoughts and faiths which cause the present difficulties.

The behavioral and cognitive psychotherapies leave the report that the thought is a vector of suffering or well-being. The consulted literature allows us to support and to confirm that the behavioral and cognitive psychotherapies are based on the principles of the scientific psychology which aim at a fast change of the feelings and the disrupted behavior.

1. 3. 1. 3. Systemic approach in family therapies

A literature review suggests that the systemic approach comes from three main sources: the theory of cybernetics (Winner, 1948), systems theory (Von Bertalanffy, 1973), and finally

[14] Ibid

the theory of communication (Bateson, 1977, 1980, and Watzlawick, et al., 1972, 1975). This approach considers the family as an open system mainly because of its constant exchanges that it shares with the environment. The definition of Bertalanffy (1973), applied to the family gives this:

> "It is a set of interdependent elements, that is to say, linked together by relations such as if one is modified, the others are also modified, and consequently the whole is transformed."

The theory holds that the history of the family affects the individual. It carries with it values, emotions and behaviors transmitted by the family from generation to generation.

Moreover, Christyne Bonneau (1991) argues that in this therapeutic approach, not only the patient is considered, but the individual and his symptoms are placed in his family and social environment. Individuals and events are studied based on their interaction than their individual characteristics. The individual is now observed in his interactional context with his family, school, work, neighborhood, friends, etc. Thus, the counselor tries to find in the interactional field of the advised person where his symptomatic behavior takes on a meaning.

1. 3. 1. 4. Humanistic approach therapies

These therapies have a lot of consideration for the human being and his abilities. In this section, we will explore the psychotherapy characteristics of Carl Ransom Rogers, one of the American Humanist psychologists, who marked his time by his valuable contribution, especially in the egalitarian concept he introduced into the therapeutic relationship. Carl Rogers introduced the notion of "Person-centered therapy." Rogers' approach believes that human beings, if supported in a meaningful and constructive way, can understand what is happening to them and to reorganize themselves.

In addition, Sinelnikoff (1993)[15] argues that Rogers' central assumption is that the individual has sufficient power to constructively deal with all aspects of his life and has the capacity for self-development, maturation, and a trend towards integration. The authors are unanimous that in this approach of Rogers, the counselor adopts a trusting and respectful attitude of the autonomy of the advised person. In Roger's approach, the person counseled is considered a client.

The approach of humanistic therapies, including the fundamental rule of Rogers, is contradictory to biblical thought. The Bible teaches us that we must not rely on our own strength, but we must cry out to God in difficult times (Ps. 107:6-7; Gn. 35:3 ; Ps. 50:15).

1. 3. 2. Christian counselling

The influence of psychology and its derivatives has given a new face to Christian counselling (Stafford, on 1969)[16]. It is important to remember that counselling is not necessarily biblical because of the requirement of biblical doctrine. Indeed, we find today that some Christian counsellors use nonbiblical approaches because they follow the footsteps of secular psychotherapists. They integrate inputs coming from their approaches, contributions coming from psychology and theology, two incompatible fields. Angelo Brusco (1983) argues that pastoral counselors have used a wide variety of therapeutic approaches.

---

[15] Sinelnikoff N., *Les psychothérapies: inventaire critique*. Paris: ESF éditeur, 1993.

[16] J. W. STAFFORD, ''Pastoral Counselling'', in Witzel, E.J., Contemporary pastoral counselling, New York: The Bruce Publishing Co. p.1-18

An interesting recent research (Mollica, 1979, p. 99) gives us an overview of the reality that prevails: the important attitudes of pastoral counsellors to the various psychiatric schools are: client-centered therapy (73%); Psychoanalysis (69.2%); Jungian theory (46%); Existential theories (40.3%); Gestalt (37.2%); and Transactional analysis (28.8%). Moreover, in the same research it is revealed that pastoral counsellors have a greater importance to psychoanalysis and behavioral therapy than any other group of mental health professionals.

We believe that profane psychotherapy cannot teach pastoral counsellors how to bring comfort, reconciliation, or healing to the soul of the Christian. Is not that a paradox? Counselling is called "biblical" when its approach is based solely on scriptural foundations in a saving perspective of the person being counseled. Indeed, the biblical help relationship is an activity that seeks faith therapy unlike psychotherapy. Through the intervention of the Holy Spirit, it enables us to listen and help our neighbor to grow in biblical faith by giving him divine love (Mt. 22 :39). It is more than the art of loving one's neighbor; it is a relationship based on trust and above all the designs of divine sanctification[17].

In today's society, different counselling alternatives are offered. Consequently, the Church of God faces a great challenge, since it is unable to meet the demand for pastoral care because of the lack of competent counsellors. Faced with this surge in psychotherapeutic offerings in the Church's universe, Christians must avoid resorting to the practice of psychotherapy to protect themselves against charlatan practices and even risks of slippage towards sectarian exploitation and financial loss. What is the specificity of biblical counselling? Pastoral care, or biblical counselling, is

---

[17] Angelo BRUSCO, *Counselling pastoral et Counselling psychologique: similitudes et différences*, (Master Essai), Ulaval, 1983.

a relationship between two or more people. Richard Baxter argues that biblical counselling permits the resolution of doubts, exposure and surrender of sins, increased knowledge of the divine Word, and all saving grace[18].

In this approach, the counsellor enters the life of the individual in distress to convince him to change and become a disciple of Jesus. Paul David Tripp divides into four parts the process of the counselling. First, the counsellor builds a healthy and biblical relationship with the counsellee[19]. The primary goal in counselling is to restore the trust relationship between the counsellee and God. In this therapy, God through Jesus, is at the center of the relationship. The counsellee is led to approach God with confidence because he will find grace and mercy (2 Jn. 1:3). Second, the counsellor collects data to understand the situation. This phase of the process allows one to capture the details of the circumstances experienced by the person being counselled. Biblical counselling is the application of the Word of God in the life of the individual. It is also a biblical awareness. Third, the counselor brings the suffering person to see himself from a divine perspective and put his trust in God's promise. Fourth, he daily applies God's intentions regarding change.

We must remember here that in the biblical counselling (pastoral counselling) spiritual direction is considered and remains a major issue. Although the person being counseled is disturbed and is seeking help, care, support, reconciliation and guidance, God remains the excellent Therapist of the situation, he alone is responsible for inner healing and spiritual growth.

---

[18] Richard BAXTER, *The Reformed Pastor*, reprinted (New York: Robert CARTER & Brothers, 1860), p. 346.

[19] Paul David TRIPP, *Instruments dans les mains du Rédempteur*, Éditions Cruciforme, p.463-493.

Let us now explain why Christians must turn to counselors who know God. In biblical counselling, in general, the Christians turn to a counsellors who knows God. When they seek healing, they must turn to the real healer who is our Lord Jesus. God is by excellence the healer of our body, spirit, and soul. God is Spirit, and where His Spirit there is healing, liberty, and deliverance. The spirit or mental disorder should be healed by the power of the Holy Spirit.

God uses the spiritual counsellor to provide help to people in crisis who turn to Him. Many Christians turn to counsellors who know God because they don't really believe in counselling which uses only psychological resources based on scientific approach and modernity.

1. 4. Dangers in counselling

In this part of our work, we will expose the dangers in counselling. Terrance Jenkins (2009) describes in his publication the dangers to be avoided in counselling. Another thing that one seeking wise counsel must understand is that there are certain inherent dangers in seeking to be counselled.

Terrance Jenkins uses the illustration of a person wishing to build a house. There are inherent dangers in the process when considering the various contractors for the job. Have they built houses for any length of time? Are they licensed by the proper authorities? What is the record of accomplishment? And so forth. Accordingly, the Bible says in, II Corinthians Chapter 10 verse 12:

> *"For we dare not make ourselves of the number or compare ourselves with some that commend themselves: but they are measuring themselves by themselves, and comparing themselves among themselves, are not wise."*

Seven of dangers that may be involved when a counselee is looking for counselor may be listed as:

1. The counsellee may be simply looking for a rubber stamp of approval.

2. The counsellee may have selective hearing. That is, he may not hear what he is being told but only what he wants to hear.

3. He may turn to the wrong kind of counsellor.

4. The problem may not be correctly identified.

5. The counsellee may have waited too long to seek help.

6. The counsellee may be seeking help from too many sources, which could bring about confusion.

7. The counsellee may be simply looking for an answer to the problem, but not finding biblical solution.

CHAPTER II:

COMPARATIVE ANALYSES OF SECULAR COUNSELLING VERSUS CHRISTIAN COUNSELLING

2. 1. Rogerian and Jay Adams approach: A comparative study

In this chapter, we will explicitly establish the notion of relationship support found within the theories presented by Carl Rogers and the approaches presented by Jay Adams. To do so, it seems necessary to briefly present the basic principles governing the concept of these authors. It is important to remember that the choice of Carl Rogers and Jay Adams in this study is not arbitrary. This is because they have respectively influenced the concept of counselling in the secular environment and in the Church.

As a first step, we will present the Person-Centered Approach which is the central element of the personality theory proposed by Carl Rogers. Second, we will explore Jay Adams' approach while emphasizing his perception of the role of the person being counseled. Finally, we will compare the main notions of the two approaches, highlighting the divergences.

2. 1. 1. The basic of Rogerian Theory

The humanist psychologist Carl Rogers developed the Person-Centered Approach in the 1940 s. This practice focuses on the client's internal resources and his / her privileged relationship with the therapist, in whom listening, and presence hold a major place[20]. In his approach, there is not a single notion of patient or sufferer, the person advised is called "client".

On the other hand, the concept of self is the core of Rogers' approach. Some notions of Rogers' therapeutic practice stem from various reflections: philosophical, existential, psychological and ethical. These different elements articulate to form the basis of the Center-on-the-Person Approach. Rogers stated:

> "The Centered-on-the-People Approach (...) is a basic philosophy rather than a simple technique or method. When this philosophy is experienced, it helps the person to increase the development of his or her abilities. When it is lived, it also stimulates constructive change in others[21]."

In this method, the emphasis is on the quality of the therapeutic relationship since it allows the client, in the interaction with the therapist, to discover for himself what he can use to find answers to his difficulties, and restore the momentum of its growth in the actualization of its competence. In the concept of Rogers' theory, there are factors that contribute to the development of the process: climate; attitudes; presence; listening and non-directivity.

2. 1. 1. 1. The Climate

This is a factor that depends on the therapist's attitude and attitude. Trust and serenity are necessary for a serene atmosphere. The Therapist's Basic Attitudes: The Person-Centered Approach exposes three basic attitudes that the therapist must possess and demonstrate to the individual who

---

[20] Rogers, C.R., Reader, Houghton Mifflin Harcourt, Boston, New York, 1989 (p. 138, free translation in French by Genevieve Odier).

[21] Ibid.p.65

consults the therapist: congruence or authenticity, positive unconditional gaze, and empathic understanding:

> *"Attitudes are expressed in responses that emphatically follow the client, the therapist's inclination to answer his questions and receive his requests, and non-systematic responses from the therapist's frame of reference. None of these behaviors violates the client's right to self-determination."*

2. 1. 1. 2. The congruence

Congruence, which according to the author, is a particularly relevant principle in the Center-on-the-Person Approach:

> *"For me to be, congruent means that I become aware of the feelings I have at that moment."*

In the field of psychotherapy congruence plays an important role as it helps to create trust and respect.

2. 1. 1. 3. The unconditional positive

The unconditional positive view is an essential attitude whose implications are security, acceptance, confidence and freedom of expression. It promotes reciprocal trust in the therapeutic relationship.

> "One of the deepest needs of people to be fully heard, totally understood and fully accepted."

2. 1. 1. 4. The empathic understanding

This attitude refers essentially to the capacity demonstrated by the therapist to understand and grasp, as adequately as possible, the inner world; the internal reference framework of his client. The therapist must grasp the experiences and emotions of his client as if they were his own. "Empathic understanding" is a way of being "in which the therapist immerses himself, in a sensitive way, in the mental universe of his client."

2. 1. 1. 5. The presence

Carl considers presence as the indispensable principle that allows growth to emerge. It opens consciousness and privileges access to a deep encounter. It allows you to connect yourself:

> "Presence as a state that makes more relevant the effectiveness of the three necessary and sufficient conditions. A state which is not an attitude, which cannot be provoked, which it settles and invades the relational space (.....) another characteristic."

2. 1. 1. 6. The Listening

This is listening attentively, what the client wants to say, what he is concerned about, bores, amuses, scares him in the present moment. A good quality listening frees the person. The individual needs the presence of another individual to become aware of his or her existence.

> "A careless listening without judgment constitutes a powerful therapeutic force even without the intention of bringing any help. It gives the individual a sense of the person, a sense of identity."

2. 1. 1. 7. The non-directivity

Rogers sees non-directivity as a careful way to remain client-centered to avoid influencing it. This attitude makes it possible to thwart the trap of dependency.

> "It is impossible for us to teach something to someone; we can only facilitate personal learning."

To conclude, Rogers' person-centered approach seeks to encourage the individual to seek out his or her true self. In this therapeutic approach, the client becomes a new person with power over herself.

2. 1. 2. Jay Adams Approach of counselling

Jay Edward Adams was born in Baltimore on January 30, 1929 and was born again five years after reading the New Testament which was given to him by a friend. Jay's work has helped thousands of pastors, students, lay people, and Christian counselors to develop a general approach to the Christian counselling and a specific response to problems. Through the Bible-led discussion, the Nouthetic approach allows the Holy Spirit to bring about changes in personality and behavior.

Jay Adams' Nouthetic approach is based on the Word of God. It considers that the Bible, the Word of God, holds divine authority, and therefore contains principles of a healthy relationship of help. On the other hand, there are several fundamental principles of Scripture that call for guidance. Each biblical hypothesis or principle relates directly or indirectly to certain aspects of the situation of the counselling.

In the concept of the approach of Jay Adams, the Holy Spirit is the main person in the interview between the counselor and the advised person. In other words, the Holy Spirit is the Counsellor (Jn. 14:16-17), the instructor and the guide of the interview.

2. 1. 3. Nouthetic counselling versus Rogerian counselling

A comparison is needed between these two approaches of counselling. We find that Rogers' approach is non-directive in relation to that of Adams, which is directive, that is, God intervenes through the counsellor. The latter exercises his authority and guides the person advised.

The fundamental presupposition of the Rogers system is perfectly compatible with liberal and humanistic thought, namely that the solution to man's problems lies in man himself. This thought is contrary to biblical theology. Man is responsible for these acts and cannot be saved by his own forces or intelligences. In this context of the biblical counselling, the notion of responsibility is important because God gives each human the ability to respond to every situation in his or her life. Jay Adams' approach in this context only confirms the doctrine of man's dependence on God. The Bible teaches us that God delivers and directs His own when they address Him in repentance (Ps. 107:6). The Rogerian approach believes that sinful man is autonomous; he does not need God, for he is himself his own solution to his problems. Moreover, the Rogerian approach uses the personal inventory data (Appendix A) and biblical verses to perform counselling (Appendix C). It seems important to make a checklist when we do biblical counselling (Appendix B).

2. 2. Secular counselling versus christian counselling

2. 2. 1. Differences and similarities

At the beginning of chapter one we dealt with what defines psychotherapy and its incompatibility with the Word of God. In the following paragraphs, we will discuss the differences and similarities between the two types of aid relationship, while giving priority to the theological aspect. In general, the Christian and secular counsellor is motivated by the same desire to help the suffering people regain their integrity and above all to overcome their problems. Moreover, the fields of action or the problems are of the same order.

Indeed, Christian counselling is distinct from secular counselling because the first specifically considers the spiritual dimension, the biblical truths, and the search for the will of God in the life of the individual. The Christian counselor understands that the Bible is the encyclopedia of life and possesses much practical wisdom about human nature, marriage and family, and human suffering. By using biblical concepts in the helping relationship, he can sometimes provide a specific direction and responsibility. In his moments of distress, the psalter (Ps. 119:24) writes:

> *"Thy testimonies also are my delight and my counsellors."*

Several Christian writers maintain that the most effective biblical counselling is the application of the Word of God to the heart of the believer, and this is the work of the Holy Spirit. In the relationship of Christian help, the counselor relates to the Church, representing the Church. He is a member of the Church and is in constant contact with her, and her practices are in principle those of the Church. Consequently, Jesus Christ through the Holy Spirit is at the center of this relationship.

In addition, the Christian counsellor and the suffering person are people of faith, people who believe in Jesus and are convinced that God will intervene in a favorable way. Unlike the secular aid relationship based on human theories, the framework for accompanying the Christian helping relationship is theological and spiritual. God is part of the process. He is the guarantor of the success of the healing process. The tools for approaching the Christian counselling are spiritual in nature: prayer, Bible reading, fraternal listening, discernment, and compassion. It is important to note that the interviews with the Christian counselor are free, in keeping with the approach of Jesus. In this Christian approach to counselling, God can use situations of distress to boast. The psalter of Psalm 118 verses 5 and 6 teaches us by this way:

> *"I called upon the Lord in distress: The Lord answered me, and set me in a large place. The Lord is on my side; I will not fear: what can man do unto me?"*

In his distress, David cried unto God, and found consolation with Him. God restores in us the disorder that we ourselves have occasioned by opening the door to sins, by giving a legal right to the enemy. Thus, Biblical counselling allows the counsellee to come closer to God, to rediscover his Christian identity and to really change his behavior, for God hates sin.

However, in the secular counselling, the counsellor helps the counsellee but is not inspired by either the Holy Spirit or the Bible. The secular counselling has an extra-biblical inspiration because it is based on theories of the humanities, and in some cases with the addition of some biblical verses to reinforce psychological principles. The wisdom of the secular aid relationship comes from men; it comes from the knowledge of the man, who thinks he finds a solution by his intelligence without divine intervention.

In biblical counselling, wisdom comes from God while man becomes the instrument of transmission of the glory of God (Ps. 23:1-3; Ps. 32:8). In secular counselling, every problem is considered as a challenge to be met, a human solution to be found, while in biblical counselling the situation is different. It is an opportunity to glorify God.

The biblical history of the healing of the man blind from birth confirms this biblical approach to the counselling. The Johannine narrative states in the Gospel of John, chapter nine, from verse 1 to 5, that Jesus saw a man who was blind from birth. His followers asked him a question saying, *"who did sin, this man, or his parents, that he was born blind? Jesus answered, neither hath this man sinned, nor his parents, but that the works of God should be made manifest in him."*

Sin may be at the root of suffering, but here it is not because sovereignty and God's goals play an important role in this affair. God permitted this suffering so that God may be glorified in the healing of the man. It is important to remember that in the biblical counselling there is a general causal relationship between sin and suffering. This approach is obviously rejected by the secular counselling.

We must remember that in the biblical approach of the helping relationship, it is the Holy Spirit of God who is, in fact, the person who advises the counsellee through the counsellor. God is therefore at the center of the relationship because of His sovereignty, His compassion, and His ability to heal the wounds of the counselee himself (Ps. 103:3). In biblical counselling, sin is the source of the problem. Therefore, the Word of God defines sin as a transgression, a disobedience to God that leads to death (Ro. 6:31-30; 18:9-20). The solution or remedy is the cross of Jesus Christ, in whom the sinner has redemption through his doctrine of repentance and sanctification.

CHAPTER III:

COUNSELLING THROUGHOUT BIBLICAL TIME

This chapter focuses on counselling through the Bible. To do this, we will present the personality of the Holy Spirit and his work. The Holy Spirit is the one who consoles, directs and guides the counselling.

3. 1. Holy Spirit and counselling

Counselling is always composed of at least three people: the human counsellor, the counsellee, and the Holy Spirit. The Holy Spirit is the great Counsellor. Through the Gospel of Matthew, chapter 18 verses 19 to 20, Jesus teaches us as follows:

> "Again I say unto you, that if two of you shall agree on earth concerning anything that they shall ask, it shall be done for them by My Father who is in Heaven. For where two or three are gathered together in My name, there am I in the midst of them."

Jesus evokes the moment when he will be present alongside his disciples, not physically but spiritually, by his Spirit. When two Christians agree sincerely, the Holy Spirit works favorably because the Spirit of Christ is with them. Two or more believers, filled with the Holy Spirit, will pray according to the will of God and not their own will; Therefore, their prayer will be answered.

3. 1. 1. The person of Holy Spirit

Several biblical passages prove the personality of the Holy Spirit. For example, in the Gospel according to John 16[22], the name *Parakletos*[23] is attributed to him. The Holy Spirit is called "Comforter" in the same way as a Jesus in 1 John 2:1. Similarly, the Spirit of God has the characteristics of a person such as the intelligence that enables him to teach all things, and to remember all that Jesus said (Jn. 14:26); to testify (Jn. 15:26; Ro. 8:16). Moreover, he is endowed with a will because he can stop a physical person from taking action (Ac. 16:7).

The Holy Spirit acts in the same way as a person because he speaks. He commands, reveals hidden things that man cannot know, struggles, creates, intercedes, restores life, to cite only these acts. In the same way, the Holy Spirit can be saddened, we can lie to him, it is the case of the biblical history of Ananias and Saphira. They have lied to the Holy Spirit and have kept for themselves some of the money they received for the land. They fell and died by the power of Holy Spirit (Ac. 5:1-11).

3. 1. 2. The works of Holy Spirit in Bible

The work of the Holy Spirit is to show the active presence of God in the world and in the Church of Jesus Christ[24]. From the history of the origin of the Church to the present

---

[22] Jn 14. 26 ; 15. 26 ; 16.7

[23] Word for Paraclete, translated by "Consoler", the one who assists, helps, defends himself, takes care of someone's interests.

[24] Wayne GRUDEN, *Théologie systématique*, Éditions Excelsis, 2010, p.699.

day, the Holy Spirit has always been the manifestation of the presence of the mighty God among His people. He, therefore, assumes the responsibility of putting on the Church of Jesus Christ, the divine power (Ac. 2:4; 17-18). In this section, we will focus more on the characteristic works because the Holy Spirit operates differently to communicate the divine blessings.

Indeed, it is the Spirit of God that strongly strengthens the inner man according to Ephesians 3 verse 16. Moreover, one of His principal activities is to purify the believer from sin and to sanctify him in his conduct. It is the power of the Spirit that sanctifies the believer (Ro. 8:4). Moreover, the Epistle of Paul to the Hebrews exhorts us to seek sanctification without which no one will see the Lord (He. 12:14).

Moreover, divine revelation is given by the Spirit of God, which confirms that all of the Holy Scriptures came into existence because men inspired by the Spirit of Christ spoke in the name of God. The Spirit is the source of divine revelation because of His ability to search the depths of God all over the earth (1 Co. 2:10).

The Holy Spirit is the source of inspiration for all divine prophecy. This act of knowledge is attributed to believers for the common good. Indeed, the Spirit has this ability to take hold powerfully of men who immediately begin to prophesy, as is the case with Saul (1 Sa. 10:10).

The Holy Spirit is responsible for the act of divine revelation. Indeed, at Pentecost, the Holy Spirit testified to the presence of God because it had come in the form of a violent wind and tongues of fire which had set on the disciples present at this divine appointment (Ac. 2:2-3). The action of the Holy Spirit through preaching also enables believers in the Church to listen to God's voice and submit to it to know His ways[25]. It is He who makes the presence of God perceptible. In him, believers can fully appreciate the manifestation of the divine presence.

One of the important works of the Spirit of God is to glorify Jesus and bear witness to him (Ac. 5:32; 1 Jn. 2:3). He convinces the world of the existence of God and the proclamation of his works. It is through the work of the Holy Spirit that the believer can confess that he is truly a child of God. He, therefore, attests the validity of the adoption of the believers by the fruit that he produces in them (Ro. 8:16).

He also gives power to believers to testify. In his earthly ministry Jesus made a promise to the apostles that they would receive the power of the Holy Spirit, indispensable to announce the truth concerning him (Ac. 1:8)[26]. The Holy Spirit has the power to intervene to struggle and destroy the works of darkness that attack the children of God. Did not Jesus tell the disciples that it is advantageous for them that He goes to God the Father to send the Holy Spirit?

Indeed, the disciples were going to be confronted with the reality of the persecution that Jesus himself had undergone in his ministry in this fallen and corrupt world. Jesus will legitimately defend his disciples by promising them the coming of an "other" Paraclete, a divine counsellor, another advocate[27]. The presence of the Holy Spirit protects, reassures, and assures the sustainability of the Church of Jesus Christ.

---

[25] By His Spirit, did not God show His ways to Moses, and His works to the children of Israel? (Ps 103. 7).

[26] The Apostles received the presence of the Holy Spirit as well as a new dimension of His power to spread the gospel of Jesus Christ to all nations.

[27] Florent, Varak, "L'Esprit dans la vie chrétienne". *La revue de théologie de la Faculté Jean Calvin*. Articles du n°260. Sommaire N° 260-mai 2011-nov. 2011-Tome LXII.

The Holy Spirit participates actively in any spiritual awakening. Finney insists on the fact that an awakening always involves a conviction of sin on behalf of the Church. According to the revivalist, Christians cannot awaken their drowsy and routine faith and immediately begin to serve God without their hearts being deeply probed by the Holy Spirit of God[28].

Likewise, all believers in Christ have received the Holy Spirit and are led by him in grace and serenity, therefore they are all sons of God, not having received a spirit of bondage (Ro. 8:15). The Bible reveals that the Holy Spirit helps the believers in their weakness and even in their distress, for they do not know what to ask in their fellowship with God.

The Bible also confirms that the Holy Spirit himself intercedes with inexpressible sighs when the believer is in a situation of physical, emotional or spiritual incapacity (Ro. 8:26). Thus, He exercises an important influence on the spirit of believers[29]. It is important to emphasize that the Holy Spirit therefore helps Christians to pray according to the divine will, that is, to ask for the things for which God Himself wants them to pray.

The role of the Spirit is also to lead and direct the believer to the ways of God. Thus, through His powerful action, the believer who walks according to the movement of the Spirit will be able to avoid evil or overcome tribulation. Paul, in his

---

[28] Charles, FINNEY, Les Réveils religieux: Discours de Charles-G. Finney. Édition M. Weber, 7eme édition, 1991, p. 5. 23

[29] Argaud ARGUES that since Pentecost, God manifests himself more personally through the intervention of the Holy Spirit in prayer: Guillaume ARGAUD, *Le Saint-Esprit et les aspects psychologiques de la foi*. La revue de théologie de la Faculté Jean Calvin. Articles n°260. Sommaire N° 260-may 2011 nov. 2011- Tome LXII.

prayer for the Ephesians, shows that it is through the work of the Holy Spirit that Christ dwells in the believer's heart through faith. In the name of Jesus, and by his expiatory work on the cross of Calvary, the Holy Spirit is the one who connects the believer to God and in communion with him.

As for spiritual gifts, the apostle Paul informs and describes in his letter to the Corinthians the origin, exercise, and utility of spiritual gifts in the church. It reveals that gifts are granted in their diversity to Christians in a sovereign and mysterious way by the Holy Spirit, independently of all personal merit, for the edification of the body of Christ (1 Co. 12:11-31). In other words, it is not the believers who personally request the gifts of the Holy Spirit, but the Spirit of God Himself distributes them according to His will.

Furthermore, J. MacArthur[30] classifies the various gifts of the Holy Spirit into two broad categories: those relating to speech and those related to service. The gifts of speech are centered on prophecy, knowledge, wisdom, teaching and exhortation, while gifts about service are oriented towards guidance, help, generosity, mercy, faith and discernment. All these spiritual gifts are intended to build the Church of Jesus Christ and to glorify God through Jesus Christ.

The manifestation of the gifts of the Holy Spirit these days is a controversial subject that sends a lot of ink into the evangelical world. This work does not claim to justify the traditional Pentecostal or charismatic position. However, we believe that spiritual gifts are now manifested in the Church of Jesus Christ. Thus, miracles and healing, languages and their interpretation, are still current and are not limited to our time. They still serve as signs not only to authenticate the authority of the men of God but also to convince the world of sin (Ac. 1:8).

---

[30] MacArhur, Nouvelle Édition de Genève 1979.

The outpouring of the Spirit at Pentecost marked the beginning of the Church of Jesus Christ. Indeed, the Bible teaches that the apostles and the hundred and twenty disciples were all filled with the Holy Spirit and began to speak other languages. The coming of the Holy Spirit that day, with supernatural signs like a fire, confirmed that God had spread His Spirit on the disciples for witness and ministry (Ac. 2:1-13; 1:8).

The fullness of the Holy Spirit enabled the disciples of the Acts of the Apostles to perform their role as witnesses of Jesus with power. Therefore, the Holy Spirit inspired the Holy Scriptures and gave to the elect the knowledge in the special revelation of God (1 Co. 2:13). The Holy Spirit is the guarantor of the Body of the Church of which Christ is the Head.

It is the Holy Spirit who ensures the existence of the Church, its protection against the dark forces[31], works according to draw men to Jesus for salvation, but faith in Jesus Christ is tributary to the work of the Holy Spirit. The Holy Spirit dwells in the Body of the Church in which he manifests the glory of God and leads him into sanctification according to the will of God.

One of the spectacular and miraculous works of the Holy Spirit is the doctrine of the divine redemption of the sinner that is possible through the Atonement of Jesus Christ. The

---

[31] The Holy Spirit is the master-worker, architect, and protector of the Church of Jesus Christ. Throughout the centuries, the history of Christianity has pointed out to us that the Church of Jesus Christ has always subsisted, and the gates of hell will never prevail against it even if it was in a sleep. About the image used in Mt. 16:13-20, by the work of the Holy Spirit, the apostle Peter was the first stone laid on the rock that is Jesus. Similarly, the Church was built on the foundation of the apostles and prophets under the direction and power of the Holy Spirit.

Apostle Paul in his letter to the Colossians (Col. 2:12-14) encourages them to express their gratitude to God the Father for having been delivered from the power of darkness and to have received salvation in Jesus Christ. Moreover, the Holy Scriptures reveal that the world is under the influence of the power of Satan. Only the power of the Trinitarian God, that of the Holy Spirit, brings about the liberation of fallen man.

3. 1. 3. The Holy Spirit in the counselling

We have just shown that the Holy Spirit is not a power but a person who acts in believers because he has the power. In counselling, the Holy Spirit is the Chief Counselor. The Holy Spirit works through the human counsellor in the counselling process. He uses the Scriptures, the sacraments, and prayers as the main vehicles through which He acts in the transformation of the believer.

Psychotherapy cannot recognize the presence and work of the Holy Spirit. This explains its failures in transformation and sanctification. True counselling implies a possible transformation and sanctification through the power of the Spirit. The results of this transformation are the fruit of the Spirit, such as love, joy, peace, patience, goodness, benignity, fidelity, gentleness, and temperance.

In the therapy of the person advised, the causes can have a demonic origin. In such a situation, human capacities remain ineffective for only the power of the Holy Spirit will enable the counsellee to achieve complete deliverance. The Bible teaches us that Jesus in His earthly ministry was filled with the power of the Spirit without measure. He chased away demons and liberated all those who were under the influence of the powers of Satan.

In biblical times, in His ministry on earth the Spirit of God was upon Jesus because He had been anointed to preach good news to the poor; He healed all who were broken in heart, and proclaimed deliverance to the captives, and the recovery of sight to the blind (Lk. 4:18). He then fulfilled the prophecy of Isaiah (Isa. 61:1).

3. 2. New covenant and counselling

Counselling is an unavoidable pastoral activity that is part of the Lord's mission. In the beginning of his earthly ministry, Jesus was anointed with the Holy Spirit at his baptism and dedicated his ministry to bringing the good news of salvation to the poor, healing people with broken hearts, proclaiming freedom to the captives of sin and deliverance to the prisoners (Lk. 4:16-21).

Indeed, the accompaniment of the suffering is demonstrated in the New Testament by examples of healing, encouragement, and consolation. Jesus came to take away the source of human suffering because by the atonement of His blood we obtain peace and divine redemption and consequently the remission of sins, which sins are the source of human suffering.

On the other hand, it is interesting to note that the Synoptic Gospels tell us that people went to Jesus Christ to seek consolation and healing. Jesus has the power to take away suffering and bring hope. All these signs, wonders and miracles were accomplished by the power of the Holy Spirit. We can establish that in the biblical counselling, it is the Holy Spirit that leads to the transformation and sanctification of the person counseled.

3. 2. 1. Jesus and Nicodemus

3. 2. 1. 1. Context of the encounter

Through the Gospel of John, we will study from a biblical perspective of counselling a passage in which Nicodemus, a lawyer received the salvation of his soul in his nocturnal encounter with Jesus.

Nicodemus, part of the imminent Jews, for the first time entered the Johannine narrative. John presents him as a Pharisee, the head of the Jews, like the one who comes to Jesus at night to talk face to face with him. The story of Jesus' encounter with Nicodemus takes place in the context of the Easter festivities.[32] In the fourth gospel, the night has a proper meaning, darkness, but in the figurative sense, it symbolizes the secret; the darkness in opposition to the light. Jesus, before his crucifixion at Golgotha, had been arrested by night with torches and lamps (Jn. 18:3).

The Johannine thought attests that Jesus is the true light that dispels darkness, fear and sin. By this light, anyone who believes in him has access to the kingdom of God. Nicodemus comes to meet Jesus at night, in secret because he had darkness in him. His belonging to the Sanhedrin explains the choice of the moment. Nicodemus being in the shadow of the night is attracted by the light of Jesus. This night encounter is therefore symbolic of the spiritual darkness in the heart of Nicodemus. In the Scriptures, "light" and "darkness" are two opposing symbols.

From an intellectual point of view, the light evokes the truth and the knowledge of the Holy Scriptures: The Word of God provides the necessary light to advance without stumbling in the faithful walk with God. Whereas "darkness" refers to error and falsehood. From a moral point of view, light evokes

---

[32] The context close to the meeting of Jesus with Nicodemus is at Jn. 2: 23-25: "Now when he was in Jerusalem at the Passover, in the feast day, many believed in his name, when they saw the miracles which he did. But Jesus did not commit himself unto them, because he knew all men, and needed not that any should testify of man: for he knew what was in man."

purity and holiness (1 Jn. 1:5) while darkness evokes sin and evil deeds.[33] (Jn. 3:19).

3. 2. 1. 2. Faith of Nicodemus and interview with Jesus

We will refer to the Word of God to understand the nature of Nicodemus' faith in counselling with Jesus. From the beginning of chapter 3 John describes Nicodemus as the secondary character. The main character is certainly Jesus, considered as the Messiah. Nicodemus is simply a prototype of Jewish leaders who hesitate and begin to believe in Jesus.

Nicodemus, a Doctor of the Holy Scriptures, in a helping relationship with Jesus, is considered an emblematic figure of inadequate faith. Nicodemus's attitude to Jesus raises the question of biblical faith. According to the Scripture, faith[34] is an attitude towards God, a sense of hope and assurance in God, an acceptance of his will. The object of faith is unique: it is God, the person and the action of God. Faith and belief are two different concepts; faith is associated with the heart and belief in thought. Belief in God is necessary to faith. This concept of faith in God does not fully answer that of Nicodemus.

Nicodemus found himself in conversation with Jesus at the sight of the miracles he was doing. The discourse of Nicodemus begins with *"Rabbi, we know that you are a Teacher came from God; for no man can do those miracles that you do, if God is not with him"*. Nicodemus claims to believe in the extent that he himself confesses his "imperfect faith" to Jesus.

---

[33] John MacArthur, *La Sainte Bible avec commentaires de John MacArthur*, Genève, Société Biblique de Genève, 1979, 1582 p.

[34] Faith is a firm assurance (*hypostasis*, translated as "person" in relation to God) and a demonstration (elenchos, from the verb elenchò, "to prove, to convince") of things hoped or not seen (He. 11:1).

This statement reveals not only a great curiosity but also an esteem and credibility on the part of Nicodemus for Jesus. Through this language, Nicodemus respects and approves the earthly ministry of Jesus because he recognizes in Jesus an anointed of the God of Israel (Jn. 3:2) as Moses.

Contrary to Nicodemus' position, Jesus in no way recognizes the legitimacy of his faith in God (Jn. 3 :3). The reasoning of Nicodemus indicates that his superficial faith is based on the miracles of Jesus and not his person.

He is impressed and convinced that the works of Jesus are divine in nature. After this counselling of Jesus with Nicodemus, he ends up believing in Jesus and becomes his disciple (Jn. 7:45-52; 19:38-42). We find, therefore, that Nicodemus passes from an immature faith to an adult faith. We can thus regard this state as an internal healing from the point of view of biblical counselling.

3. 2. 1. 3. Development of the character of Nicodemus

At the beginning of his encounter with Jesus, Nicodemus demonstrated that his faith was superfluous. It is a faith that is based solely on signs and miracles. Jesus knew the sufferings of Nicodemus. He needed spiritual therapy. This is not a matter of the human mind and of an intellectual or physical effort (Jn. 3:6). Only the redemption of his soul (the birth of water and the Spirit) could solve the spiritual difficulties of Nicodemus (Jn. 3:3).

For John MacArthur, the expression "born of water and of the Spirit" would mean in Johannine thought a spiritual purification of the soul accomplished by the Holy Spirit through the Word of God.

3. 2. 1. 4. Christocentric principles for Counselling

The Christocentric principles for Counselling are defined as the approach of the counselling centered on Jesus. We can see that in this relationship of help, Jesus Christ is the main character. John also points out that Nicodemus went to Jesus at night for a special conversation (Jn. 3:1-2). In this Gospel of John, those who saw in Jesus the Son of God always came to him to seek consolation[35].

But Jesus has no intention of entering a discussion with Him. Jesus, knowing the heart and the root of the problem of Nicodemus, answers rather the essential question that Nicodemus refuses to ask (Jn. 3:3) concernant regeneration and spiritual transformation by the Spirit of God.

Jesus reveals to Nicodemus the divine truths and spiritual realities of the new birth (Jn. 3:10) and offers him salvation which is the true solution to his ills. The approach of Jesus in this relationship with Nicodemus is to make him grow and to help him reach spiritual maturity. Jesus uses a simple but strategic approach.

First, Jesus welcomes Nicodemus when the latter comes by night seeking to know who he is. (Jn. 3:21). Second, Jesus read Nicodemus's heart and analyzed his needs to discern that the specific problem of Nicodemus was at the level of his inner person (soul, spirit, and heart). Third, Jesus questions Nicodemus' assurance and does not trust his external person (Jn. 3:9, 10).

Fourth, despite the confrontation demonstrated by his lack of understanding and ignorance of the things of the Spirit, Jesus continues his journey to bring Nicodemus back to that which is spiritual and to the obedience of the divine Word.

---

[35] Jesus and the paralytic in Jn 5.1-9; The marginal Samaritan woman in Jn 4.7-42.

Throughout this approach, Jesus demonstrates patience and empathy while remaining authentic.

3. 2. 2. Jesus and the woman caught in adultery (Jn. 8: 1-11)

Adultery is a sexual relationship between a married person and another person other than the spouse, whether married or not. It is a breach of the promise of fidelity that the man or woman gave at the time of his marriage. Adultery destroys family cohesion and establishes hatred. Moreover, adultery is an intentional act, and the expression of the intention of the heart. Acts are the fruit of man's thoughts and will. Therefore, the Bible teaches that evil thoughts and adulteries come from the heart (Mt. 15:19; Mk. 7: 21).

The God who instituted marriage hates the sin of adultery. In Moses' law, adultery was severely punished with death for both involved. Leviticus 20:10 clearly states this:

> "If there is a man who commits adultery with another man's wife, one who commits adultery with his friend's wife, the adulterer and the adulteress shall surely be put to death."

The most holy God never changed his position on marriage and adultery even in the New Covenant. Both in the Old Testament and in the New Testament, adultery is considered a serious sin, a transgression to the divine law, a provocation of divine wrath.

The Gospel of John reports a case in which a woman was caught in the act of adultery (Jn. 8:1-11). This story takes place in the time of Jesus, therefore in the New Testament period when the Mosaic Law on the sin of adultery was still applied.

In this study, we will explore how Jesus deals with the problem or how he advises this woman in crisis situations. From a theological point of view, this crisis is obviously linked to the breakdown of communion in the relationship with God. Jesus' counselling approach is a directive, practical and direct.

Indeed, Jesus finds himself confronting the Pharisees who set him a trap by presenting him with a case of adultery. It was a woman caught in the act of adultery. Jesus confirms the sentence of Moses before his detractors but lays down one and only condition for its execution: *"Let him who is without sin cast the first stone."* When they heard this condition, they withdrew. Jesus then remained alone with the woman for a helping relationship. Jesus did not judge her based on the accusations, but he was compassionate, tolerant, reassuring, and understandable. In this crisis, Jesus identified the risks. For him, the way of understanding the action of others is decisive in the search for consolation. She is responsible for her act, but Jesus does not condemn her, he understands her emotions and manages them. This woman did not sin against the people who wanted her death, but she transgressed the divine law, so she sinned against God alone, and she did what was evil in his eyes so that God was right in His sentence and without reproach in his judgment (Ps. 51:4).

Jesus was listening attentively to this woman who was taken hostage by hypocritical accusers. John makes no mention of the man involved in this grave sin of adultery. As defined above, the act of adultery involves two persons. In this story there is only one person who is charged. This means that the real intention of the scribes and Pharisees was not to know who committed this act, but their intention was to trap Jesus in this crisis.

Jesus avoided the condemnation of this woman and became interested in her change of attitude when He henceforth declares that he does not condemn her, but he gives her the recommendation not to sin again. Jesus said to the woman *"go, and sin no more."* This has a great significance in the helping relationship. Jesus listened attentively to the woman, directed her in her suffering, understood her inner emotions and helped her find the path to inner healing.

The counsel given by Jesus to this woman aims at a change of attitude to have a life of consecration in the Lord. In such a situation, counselors should not judge the situation but rather create conditions of trust and an environment of love and avoid confrontation with the person advised. It is the Word of God through the Holy Spirit that challenges the sinner. The teaching of Jesus draws our attention to remind us that the counselor must focus on the person in crisis, but he does not focus on the problem because the solution of the problem lies in the sincere application of the Word of God which imposes an inner change.

3. 2. 3. Jesus and the Samaritan Woman (Jn. 4: 1-42)

The story of the Samaritan woman reinforces the concept of biblical counselling and especially confirms the divinity of Jesus. This biblical passage also emphasizes Jesus' immeasurable love for the world, whatever their social status. In this part of our study, we will focus on the meeting of Jesus with the Samaritan woman in a counselling perspective. How does Jesus succeed in freeing this woman despite the social barrier between the Jews and the Samaritans?

The narrative of the Samaritan woman leads us to believe that God had programmed the deliverance of this woman who experienced much humiliation, shame and contempt because of her social condition. The way in which the Evangelist John explains how Jesus went to Samaria (Sychar) allows us to argue that Jesus was giving much consideration to the marginalized. I will say that it was the Holy Spirit who guided him to this suffering soul.

Counsellors must be guided by the Holy Spirit in all decisions taken to conduct the interview. Moreover, they must be ready to move everywhere, beyond the walls of the church. Jesus sensed an urgent need in the city of Sychar, and without hesitation he went there. God often creates circumstances allowing his children to return to his divine plan.

Indeed, a woman from Samaria comes alone to draw water from the well of Jacob and meets Jesus, a meeting that will change her life (Jn. 4:7). In the tradition of the time, women generally came to draw water in groups, early or late enough to avoid the heat of the day. Some biblical commentators think that if the Samaritan woman had come alone, it was probably because the shame of her condition kept her isolated from other women. The fact that Jesus is alone with this woman shows that this is a divine encounter in God's plan. Similarly, counselling is an encounter with the Holy Spirit because one goes there to find a divine solution where humans with their intelligence cannot find lasting answers.

John clearly states in verse 7 that Jesus asks this woman for a drink. This attitude is unacceptable and an unusual offense in the tradition of the time. In pastoral counselling, the counsellor should not take account of tradition and its barriers, but it is God who takes care of it. God is more than tradition. The Jews have no relationship with the Samaritans, but Jesus goes beyond these considerations because he is sent to heal those with broken hearts (Lk. 4:18).

Jesus used the physical needs of this woman, who wanted water from the well to help her support life in this arid region, to teach a lesson on things describing her spiritual need. Jesus could establish a contact with this woman which led her to take cognizance of her spiritual need (Jn. 4:14, 15). Jesus focuses on the spiritual need for the conversion and purification of sin. Jesus knows the intimate life of this woman, a depraved life. In the interview, Jesus used patience to reach the real problem of this woman (several husbands, instability, depravity, problem of commitment). Jesus shows us that counsellors must be patient while listening attentively. It is in this attitude that the Holy Spirit reveals to us hidden things. Only spiritual inspiration allows us to know the hidden things that nobody knows.

Moreover, the first contacts in a counselling cannot lead to knowing the real problem of the individual. The purpose of Jesus in this counselling is to change her attitude and receive inner healing. Jesus finally reveals His Messiah to this woman, this knowledge influenced her so much that she went into the city to tell people to come and see a man of influence, the Messiah. In this story, we can conclude that the Samaritan woman came to Jesus and found restoration by her attitude change about her own condition and the Master.

3. 2. 4. Jesus transforms the life of Zacchaeus

The story of Zacchaeus' encounter with Jesus is striking and sends a clear message to Christians in counselling about the attitude to be observed in biblical counselling with rich people. We will analyze the passage of Luke 19 verses 1 to 10, outlining the counselling approach used by Jesus for the salvation of a rich man called Zacchaeus. Indeed, Zacchaeus was a rich man, who organized the collection of taxes on behalf of the Romans. His social status gave him uncontested authority and influence. Despite his small size, Zacchaeus was one of the great, but his soul was lost. A lost soul is a soul that has no life in Jesus Christ (Jn. 11:25), therefore a soul without salvation. It is a tormented soul. Despite his wealth, and his social position, Zacchaeus had internal sufferings which his riches could not satisfy. Zacchaeus lived in fraud and dishonesty (Lk. 19: 8). The wisdom of God teaches us in Proverbs 28 verse 6 that it is better for the poor who walks in his integrity, than the one with tortuous ways and who is rich. The love of money or of goods acquired in a dishonest way leads man to perdition. What good is it for a man to steal all the wealth of the people if he loses his soul? (Mk. 8: 36).

Considering our analysis, we can deduce that Zacchaeus had a problem of attitude and needed a real change to be at peace. This transformation was possible only after his encounter with Jesus Christ. In this counselling, Jesus knew what this man was suffering. We will analyze the stages of Jesus' encounter with Zacchaeus to try to deduce the few Christological principles for counselling. Zacchaeus is an emblematic figure of treacherous Jews, and crooks that get rich on the backs of their fellow citizens to satisfy the needs of the Romans. Indeed, Zacchaeus had certainly heard of Jesus Christ, a man of influence who performed many miracles and healings.

The Evangelist Luke reports that Jesus, accompanied by a host of pilgrims, crossed the city of Jericho to go to Jerusalem for the Passover. Zacchaeus sought to see who Jesus was, but he failed because of the crowd (Lk. 19:2). Despite the barrier of the crowd, he will be able to meet Jesus at home (Lk. 19:5). When God plans to deliver us and we resolve to meet him intimately, no barrier can stop us. In his love, and in his sense of discernment, Jesus decided to meet Zacchaeus at home despite his bad reputation. The presence of Jesus in the life of Zacchaeus brought joy and peace. Jesus accepts without discrimination all those who come to Him (Rev. 3: 20).

Like Jesus, the Counsellor must avoid prejudice and pray for spiritual discernment to recognize the real needs of the delinquent. The love of people and intensive listening are key factors in the success of biblical counselling. In his compassion for Zacchaeus, Jesus did not consider Zacchaeus' wealth or bad reputation to lead him to salvation. He simply considered that Zacchaeus should be transformed, that a soul should be saved so that God the Father might be glorified. Jesus loved Zacchaeus, but he hated his attitude, that is, his sins. In the theology of biblical counselling, sin is the source of evil (1 Co. 6:18). Therefore, sin must be removed from the life of the counsellee. This is impossible for man, but in Jesus Christ, we do it.

The presence of Jesus in Zacchaeus changed his heart to such an extent that he announced on his own initiative to give half of what he possessed to the poor and that he would give quadruple to all those to whom he had done wrong (Lk. 19:5, 6). The moment spent with Jesus really changed and transformed his life. Jesus had influence because he was anointed with the Holy Spirit. His presence in the house of Zacchaeus changed the course of events in the life of Zacchaeus. Counselling should provide a climate of peace, joy, and security, that is, the counsellor should be called to perform this type of ministry in the church. Because the Bible declares that the Lord is the Spirit; and where the Spirit of the Lord is, there is freedom (2 Co. 3:17). Jesus, by the power of the Spirit, brought freedom and new life to Zacchaeus. The goal of biblical counselling is to seek and save those who are lost by confronting them with the Word of God.

CHAPTER IV:

THE HUMAN BEING, ITS TRIPARTITE NATURE AND DISEASES

4. 1. Biblical conception of the components of the human being

Before presenting some notions illustrating how the understanding of physical, emotional, mental and demonic diseases is expressed, it is essential to illuminate the tripartite anthropology in the Bible that distinguishes the body (sôma), the soul (psyche) and the spirit (pneuma). We are interested here in the biblical conception of the components of the human being because the Bible (Jb. 1-2) reveals to us the fundamental principle of spiritual warfare found in the spiritual world. According to this principle, all battles in life, whether physical, spiritual, emotional, mental, financial, or against human personalities, are only external manifestations of a spiritual cause.

The anthropology of the apostle John distinguishes between the flesh and the spirit, the life of the soul and the life of the spirit. John's conception of the man is not dualistic but rather tripartite (Fromaget, 2000). In Paul's case, the anthropological tripartition is evident. The tripartite comprehension of the human being becomes more precise in 1Thessalonians chapter 5, verse 23, then Paul writes:

"May the God of peace make you completely holy and may he keep you perfectly spirit, soul and body so that you may be blameless when our Lord Jesus Christ comes."

Moreover, it is important to note that the divine commitment of the sixth chapter of Deuteronomy, in verse 5, taken up in the synoptic gospels (Mt. 22:37; Mk. 12:30; Lk. 10:27) explicitly refers to the tripartite comprehension " mind, soul and body".

4. 1. 1. Body (sôma) of the human being

The human body is part of God's creation. It is the physical or material part of man, it is the part that is in contact with the material world. The body is made of flesh (Pr. 5:11) and is the death part of man (Ro. 6:12). The material Character of Man makes him an earthly, fragile and temporary being who depends on the Holy God for his existence (Ps. 56:4). Man remains in this body as long as he is on earth (2 Co. 5:9), but this corruptible body will return to the earth (Gn. 3:19, Ec. 3:20, Jb. 1:21). It is because of sin that the body must die (Ro. 8:10). Life can only be attained by the Spirit (Ro. 8:14). The body is the place where the mind resides. Among Christians, the Holy Spirit makes it a temple (1 Co. 6:19).

Moreover, the soul and the spirit are the spiritual parts that allow man to act, to think, to feel, to react emotionally, and to respond spiritually to God. Mary's words confirm this concept when she expresses herself in this way in the first chapter of Luke's Gospel in verses 47 and 48:

"My soul exalts the Lord, and my spirit rejoices in God, my Savior."

We can notice that this passage of Luke evokes the two (spiritual) components of the human being, that is, the soul and the spirit.

4. 1. 2. Soul of the human being

In the Hebrew Bible "Nephesh" is one of the words translated by soul. The Greek equivalent in the Septuagint and the New Testament is Psyche in Greek. The word Nephesh, which can be translated in many other ways, most often as a living being, breathes life (Gn 1:20, 2:7, 1 Co. 15:45). One of the fathers of the Church, Tatien, argues that support that the human soul is by nature mortal, but it is also capable of not dying. Fromaget (2000) points out that the Christian image affirms that the soul and body come from the same creation, and both belong to the created world. They then form an inseparable unit (Gn. 2:7). It is the natural man who is composed of a body and a soul and who is condemned to disappear if he cannot receive the spirit (Ro. 8:12).

The word "soul" refers to the intangible part of human beings (Mt. 10:28, Ps. 19:8). The soul of the human being is therefore the faculty that we cannot see or touch and which nevertheless makes us feel, think, want and act. In the Epistles of the Apostle Paul, the soul is opposed to the spirit; the spiritual man being the one who lives, through Christ, a new life. Several passages from the Bible show that the soul is considered as the seat of personal life. Sin puts the soul in great danger of perdition (Eze. 18:4).

4. 1. 3. Human spirit

The Bible confirms that Man is endowed with a spirit. It teaches us that men or women whose human spirit is so welcoming and open that the Holy Spirit can literally fill them. This is the case of John the Baptist who was filled with the Holy Spirit from his mother's womb (Lk. 1:15);

of Elizabeth who heard Mary's greeting, her child jumping into her womb, and she was filled with the Holy Spirit (Lk. 1:41); of Zechariah, when he was filled with the Holy Spirit and began to speak as a prophet (Lk. 1.67) Jesus, filled with the Holy Spirit, came back from the Jordan, and was led by the Spirit into the wilderness (Lk. 4:1); Peter, filled with the Holy Spirit, spoke to the leaders of the people, and elders of Israel, (Ac. 4:8); and at Pentecost, where the disciples were all filled with the Holy Spirit, and began to speak in other languages, as the Spirit gave them to speak.

Moreover, the human mind could contemplate and penetrate the mysteries of God. It is through the spirit and only through this component of the human being that natural man can be reborn as a child of God (Jn. 1:12-14). Jesus reminds us that it is the Spirit who gives life, that is, the flesh is of no use because his words are spirit and life (Jn 6:69). The spirit is the faculty by which man transforms himself into the one who inhabits him and thus spiritualizes, fulfills and completes himself. Without the human spirit, the Spirit of God cannot be welcomed into man. The apostle John, being a theologian, believes that God is Spirit, those who worship must worship Him in spirit and in truth (Jn. 4:24). Another revealing passage in the second chapter of Genesis verse 2 confirms that man has a spiritual component, when God created man from the dust of the earth, he breathed into his nostrils a breath of life and man became a living being (Gn. 2:7).

4. 2. Human being and the diseases

Through our research, we do not claim to provide medical advice directly or indirectly. Nor do we claim to make a diagnosis directly or indirectly. The theories or knowledge contained in this study are for information purposes only, for academic use, as possibilities of investigating a spiritual state in order to help the suffering person, the biblical counsellor to better understand the origin of his health problems.

The purpose of this session is to present some concepts illustrating how the understanding of different sufferings in relation to the components of the human being is expressed. When we speak of illness or suffering, we are referring to any spiritual, mental, emotional, or physical condition that could have a negative impact on the human body, soul and spirit. We distinguish five main types: spiritual illness, physical illness, emotional illness, mental illness, demonic states. But we will focus on a few in our study.

4. 2. 1. Spiritual illness

Sin is a spiritual sickness and an offence to God, that is, a deliberate transgression of His law (1 Jn. 3:4). Sin is the responsibility of men. It is important to note that there is a difference between committing a sin and living in sin. The lives of biblical heroes show how even those who are called by God and who are faithful to Him in His service do not sometimes escape sin. But they do not cherish an evil in which they would be pleased and that they choose to commit.

Sin leads to spiritual death and is therefore contrary to the sovereign will of God. Chapter 3 of the book of Genesis reveals to us that it was through Adam that sin entered the world, death also entered through him; and thus, death came to all men, because all sinned. When the transgression is not treated, it even affects all the offspring (Ro. 5.12). The Word of God declares that the wage of sin is death (Ro. 6:23a). Indeed, death reigned from Adam to Moses, even over those who had not sinned by a transgression like that of Adam (Ro. 5:14). Spiritual illness cannot be treated by medical science because it is within the sovereignty of God. God is Spirit, sin is a spiritual disease that directly affects the spiritual components of the human being (soul, spirit), it is through the power of the Holy Spirit that sin can be annihilated.

Sin also weakens the spirit and is accompanied or will be followed by grief and suffering. Sin, if it is unforgiven and not eradicated, will destroy the soul. Healing for this type of illness comes from repentance, forgiveness of sins and acceptance of Jesus Christ as Lord and personal Savior. The Bible warns that he who hides his transgressions can never prosper, but if he confesses and renounces them, he will obtain mercy (Pr. 28:13).

4. 2. 2. Physical illness

Diseases are an alteration of the functions or health of a living organism that affects everyone, the righteous, the wicked, the rich and the poor. They can result from organic disorders that are problems that doctors can observe and detect. Physical illnesses can also result from functional disorders that result from a dysfunction of an organ or part of the body. Functional disorders include a variety of conditions in which a problem in one part of the body disrupts the entire body. The most common are heart disease, high blood pressure, diabetes, peptic ulcers and allergies. Because of the integrated nature of man, disease in one part of the body affects the whole body. This means that functional diseases that evolve without being controlled can lead to organic diseases. The Bible tells us several obvious examples of physical illnesses, paralyzed, lame (Ac. 3:1-26) and many cases of deafness (Mk. 9:25-29), blindness (Gn. 27:1; Jn. 9:1-3) or mutism (Lk. 1:2-23; 64:67-68), skin disorders such as leprosy (Lk. 17:11-14).

4. 2. 3. Emotional illness

Emotional illnesses result from harmful emotions such as anger (Ps. 37:8, Eph. 4:26), hatred (Gn. 37:4), bitterness (He. 12:15), anxiety (Ps. 107:13-16) etc. Healing in this case comes through both vertical and horizontal forgiveness. Vertical forgiveness occurs when you ask God to forgive you for the guilty emotions. When you repent, God heals these inner conditions. Horizontal forgiveness and healing take place when you forgive those who have offended you. Some people call this "inner healing". The apostle Paul teaches us the importance of forgiveness in the Christian life. Most of the Christians in the Church of Colossae were from paganism. The apostle exhorts them to support each other and recommends that if one has reason to complain about the other, they should forgive each other. Just as Christ forgave them, they must also forgive themselves (Co. 3:13). Forgiveness is therefore a power that delivers and heals.

4. 2. 4. Mental illness

Mental illness is defective mental health caused by mental deficiency, illness, nervous depression, birth defects, and psychological states not caused by a demonic presence. However, the Stanford study (2017)[36] on the evaluation of the attitudes and beliefs of Christians with mental illness reveals that mental illness was from demonic sources. In the Bible, Saul seems to have been affected by a melancholic psychosis with homicidal crises (1Sa. 16:14, 19:9, 22:17). To Nebuchadnezzar, are attributed the symptoms of temporary lycanthropy (Dan. 4:33):

> "The same hour was the thing fulfilled upon Nebuchadnezzar: and he was driven from men, and did eat grass as oxen, and his body was wet with the dew of heaven, till his hairs were grown like eagles' feathers, and his nails like birds' claws."

---

[36] Matthew S. STANFORD, Demon or disorder: A survey of attitudes toward mental illness in the Christian church. Journal of Mental Health, Religion & Culture, Vol. 10 (5), 2007, p. 445-449.

After seven years of humiliation, God led the king to no longer raise his Heart with pride, but rather to look up to heaven in submission. God responded with compassion and restored his mental health. Mental illness is a spiritual reality.

4. 2. 5. Demonic conditions

Demonic spirits can be the cause of persecution and disease in humans. The Bible tells us that Jesus gave power (dunamis in Greek : δύναμις) and authority (exousia in Greek : ἐξουσία) over all demons, as well as overall diseases (Lk. 9:1). There are hundreds of people bound by Satan to diseases with demonic causes. There are hundreds more suffering from oppression, possession and obsession at the hands of the enemy. If this were the case, it means that there are satanic spirits who can possess, oppress and obsess the human being.

4. 2. 5. 1. Demonic possession

The Greek word δαιμονίζομαι (Daimonizomai) means "to be under the power of a demon". Demons can possess human beings. Indeed, demonic possession is a condition in which one or more impure spirits inhabit the body of a human being. By living there, they completely control it (Mk. 9:17, Lk. 4:33, Mt. 4:24). Experiences of demonic possession are on the increase in the United Kingdoms[37]. Demonic possession is a reality of which the Church is aware. Demonic demonstrations and its testimonies prove that impure spirits are active nowadays. War is spiritual, it can only be won by the power of Jesus Christ, by the anointing of the Spirit of God. The dramatic story of the demonic man in the land of the Gerasenes (Mk 5:1-20) illustrates this reality and shows us how great the mental imbalance of some possessed could

[37] Kirsty ROWAN and Karen DWYER, *"Demonic possession and deliverance in the diaspora: phenomenological descriptions from Pentecostal deliverees"* Journal of Mental Health, Religion & Culture, Vol. 18 (6), 2015, p. 440-455.

be. Sometimes these mental disorders were accompanied by physical disabilities: autism (Mt. 9:32); deafness and autism (Mc: 9:25); blindness and autism (Mt. 12:22); epilepsy (Mt. 17:14-18, Mc: 9:14-27, Lk. 9:37-43). The acts of the apostles mention a woman possessed by a spirit of divination (Ac. 16:16). She was delivered in the name of Jesus. Jesus' ministry was unique. Jesus' method of healing was different from that of Jewish exorcists of his time. Jesus cast out demons by His Word (Mt. 8:16) and not by magical incantations. In this story we notice that he shows compassion and love for this person in distress. The deliverance of the possessed persons was one of Jesus' missions in his earthly ministry (Lk. 4:18).

The true Christian cannot be possessed, for his body is the temple of the Holy Spirit who cannot cohabit with unclean spirits. The apostle Paul wrote to the Corinthians :

> "What? know ye not that your body is the temple of the Holy Ghost which is in you, which ye have of God, and ye are not your own? For ye are bought with a price: therefore glorify God in your body, and in your spirit, which are God's."
> (1 Co. 6:19)

The apostle Paul describes the reality of the Christian : his body is inhabited by the Holy Spirit. To avoid this demonic state, the Christian is called to put his body at the service of the glory of the Lord (Ro. 12:1-2)[38].

---

[38] Ro. 12 :1-2: I beseech you therefore, brethren, by the mercies of God, that ye present your bodies a living sacrifice, holy, acceptable unto God, which is your reasonable service. And be not conformed to this world: but be ye transformed by the renewing of your mind, that ye may prove what is that good, and acceptable, and perfect, will of God.

4. 2. 5. 2. Demonic oppression

Evil spirits can oppress the people. The verb " to oppress " in the word "to oppress" means to come on, to come against or to bind from the outside. This oppression is accomplished by evil spirits in various ways. They cause depression, create negative circumstances and put evil thoughts in the mind such as thoughts of suicide, immorality, disbelief, fear, etc. Demons create satanic circumstances and situations that tempt man to sin: Christians too can be oppressed. If demonic powers bind people in oppression from the outside. The Bible tells us that Jesus untied an oppressed woman in the synagogue of the spirit of infirmity. Evil spirits can oppress the human being. The conduct of Christians can be satanically directed if they let demonic forces oppress them. Believers, through their own actions, can "give access" or make room for Satan to use them (Eph. 4:27).

God anointed Jesus Christ with the Holy Spirit and strength to heal all those who were under the power of the devil (Ac. 10:38). The Bible counselor should apply Jesus' way of doing things to free the oppressed Christian.

4. 2. 5. 3. Obsession

The word "obsession" comes from the verb "obsess" which translates the state of a person whose thought is inspired by the devil or his demons, in order to distance him from God. In this condition she becomes obsessed with an interest or concern for demons. This is an unusual interest in the occult sciences, demons and Satan, who controls interests and activities in a dictatorial way. Possession and obsession are two different states. In possession, the satanic spirit is inside the body while in obsession, the demon is supposed to act outside. He who is obsessed with the things of the world moves away from the face of God. The apostle John mentions (1Jn. 2 :15-16) : Love not the world, neither the things that are in the world. If any man love the world, the love of the Father is not in him. For all that is in the world, the lust of the flesh, and the lust of the eyes, and the pride of life, is not of the Father, but is of the world.

CHAPTER V:

CHRISTIAN IMMIGRANT AND COUNSELLING IN LOCAL CHURCH

5. 1. Christian immigrant and Faith

5. 1. 1. Loss of faith, a source of trouble for Christian immigrants.

In this text, we will try to understand why the challenges facing society can impact the faith of Christian immigrants and in particular how biblical counselling can help these people to maintain their life in Christ in the face of the bad weather of life in the country of adoption. It would be interesting to first understand what the Bible says about immigration. The Hebrew Bible reveals that God created the earth and everything on it and also created man in his image so that they would live together to worship Him (Gn. 1:27,2:7).

Thus, God has given human beings the ability or willingness to explore and discover the expanse of the earth. This is why, for reasons of persecution, war, natural disaster or social instability, human beings always seek to enter a foreign country to settle in the hope of finding a better life. The Old Testament illustrates many examples of biblical characters or immigrant populations. The first book of the Pentateuch teaches us that Terah and his family left Ur for Canaan, but finally settled in Charan (Gen. 11:31). Likewise, Abram left his country by faith and arrived in Canaan where the Lord God had made a covenant with him (Gn.12:1).

In addition, Joseph was sold by his brothers for twenty pieces of silver to the Israelites who deported him against his own will to Egypt (Gn. 37:28). In addition, during the 400 years spent in Egypt, God's people were enslaved in Egypt and then delivered by God through Moses. The books of 2 Kings, 2 Chronicles, Ezra and Nehemiah also speak of the exile of the Jews of Jerusalem and the Kingdom of Judah to Babylon under Nebuchadnezzar II. God used Babylon as a judgment of Israel because of its idolatry and rebellion against it. The people of Israel like Abram, Joseph and deported prophets like Daniel and Ezekiel had confidence in God during their stay in the foreign country. These biblical heroes had faith in God despite the great challenges. They could have given up and moved away from the face of God, but they remained faithful and honest to God. God alone delivers His people when they pray and seek His face and turn away from their evil ways (Ps 3:4; 2Ch. 7:14). The biblical contexts mentioned above reveal some similarities with those of Christian immigrants both in terms of social challenges and prospects for personal success.

Indeed, Christian immigrants to Canada, who come to Canada for a long stay or to settle there like any immigrant, face many changes in their lives, including divorce or separation, psychosomatic illnesses and anxiety disorders, domestic violence, recurrent unemployment, racism, etc. All this can be attributed to poor adaptation or difficult acculturation leading to the gradual abandonment of the Christian faith. The challenges are so great in the host country that the more fragile Christians are moving away from the face of God.

Despite societal pressure and personal challenges, a minority of immigrants nevertheless choose to walk sincerely with

God, refusing to conform to the present century, to embark on the path of religious syncretism and immorality and to advocate self-centeredness (Mt 6:33). Even in the worst of situations, God maintains a faithful minority, that is, courageous, honest, just and incorruptible men and women to make his truth known (2 Ch. 19:31). God does not seek men and women, floating and carried away by any wind of doctrine, by the deceit of men, by their cunning in the means of seduction.

5. 2. Case study in a local church: Helping a demon troubled person through counselling

5. 2. 1. Research methodology

Our study required us to go into the area to collect information from the people who have experienced the counselling in the church. By methodology we mean our way of collecting data or information both from our personal experience in our church and from other pastors. We have therefore developed steps in the process to be followed. At the beginning of our research, the difficulty was how to get to a certain amount of information; how to explore Christian immigrant support programs, churches and their pastors to understand the facts of biblical counselling.

Our concern in this work is not to do scientific research in the strictly sense of the term, but to produce an honest and credible study on the significance of biblical counselling in the healing and recovery of the suffering soul. We do not invent anything in our research nor do we pretend to invent the wheel, our contribution to research is intended to contribute to the well-being of Christians. It was essential for us to learn a minimum of reference work on the subject of biblical counselling. At regular intervals, we have set aside time for personal reflection and exchanges of views with experienced evangelical pastoral colleagues. The particularity of our work is very relevant to the Christian immigrant community, whose needs for biblical counselling are growing.

5. 2. 2. Criteria for participation and conduct of the interview or survey

The interviews, which have been undertaken in recent years, have been conducted in two types of intervention. The first step was to look at the people we followed in the local church. The second type of intervention focused on the practice of pastors in biblical counselling. With regard to the number of counsellors or pastors interviewed as part of our work, it was not very important for us to obtain a strictly representative sample of the population studied.

We have observed a lot of our own experiences with our faithful and have sought the input of some pastors from Quebec City. This choice was made because we believe that these pastors are very open-minded and have expressed their interest in the biblical helping relationship. The practical difficulty of having a very large number of cases does not in any way affect the results of our study. The number was relatively minor to us, as long as we were interested in analyzing the quality of the content of the counselling sessions. In this type of interview, in which qualitative analysis is more important than quantitative analysis, we estimate the number of five to ten interviews to be sufficient. We defend this approach so far as in a relationship of biblical help, there are several meeting sessions.

5. 2. 3. Living stories: Pastoral counselling in church context

5. 2. 3. 1. Case study #1: Helping a demon-possessed person

This story is a real story that we lived in our church. We will try to establish here various stages of the process of pastoral accompaniment that have allowed us to lead a person in a crisis to Christ. On Sunday, March 1, 2015, we had a visit from a pastor in his sixties, accompanied by his wife, to share the Word of God with our church. This pastoral couple, with whom we are making our way in pastoral ministry, are disciples of Christ, reflect love and compassion for troubled souls.

Indeed, after completing the morning worship and going into some occupations with Pastor Bernard, we decided together to sit down to dinner for supper at our private residence in Quebec City. At about 9:00 pm, meals were served, and we were ready to eat when the phone rang. I took it myself to go in line with my interlocutor. She was a Christian Baptist woman in her forties. She begged me to go to her sister because of her niece, about twenty-one years of age, who was in a critical situation requiring spiritual help.

On the other hand, we were a little surprised when she insisted on her request. "My niece is in a critical state of spiritual crisis; she does not want to go to the hospital and she asks to meet a pastor" she said. The woman and her niece are not an integral part of our local assembly and the relations that bind us are friendly. We had quickly analyzed the situation and had chosen not to eat. We had then obeyed the Holy Spirit and we went to her home within five minutes.

When we went to the young woman's house, we met her mother who briefly explained the situation. She pointed out that her daughter was about to sleep on her bed in her room when suddenly she began a crisis. We went back to the young woman's room with her mother, and we tried to address her a few words, but we failed because her crisis persisted.

We observed in the young lady behavioral disorders and a feeling of persecution that could go as far as a point of irrationality and delirium. She threw herself and crawled on the floor of her room screaming. During her behavioral troubles, we drew her attention to us. As I prayed using the name of Jesus and the blood of Jesus, Pastor told her to repeat "Jesus!". She had difficulty in obeying, many difficulties in saying so until the pastor told her to repeat Revelation chapter 12: 11.

> "And they overcame him by the blood of the Lamb, and by the word of their testimony; and they loved not their lives unto the death."

She repeated, then, following the repetition of the verse, she began to say, "thank you, Jesus." And her spirit returned to her. She pledged to follow Jesus as her Savior and Lord. We advised her mother to make her sit down and give her to drink. We have only used the name of Jesus, the blood of Jesus and the Word of God under the inspiration of the Holy Spirit to drive back the adversary.

The brothers and sister of the young were joyful and greeted us with dignity. The next day I received a phone from the aunt of the young woman thanking me and informing me that her niece had slept well in the night and that she is in good health.

Saturday following the day of the event, as the senior pastor of the church, I gave an interview to the young woman accompanied by her father. The purpose of this meeting was to collect information related to her religious and family background, to explain the meaning of the tests and then to propose a customized spiritual journey. In our interview, the father confessed to me that she is not yet baptized with water despite her occasional attendance of churches.

The young woman agreed to come every Saturday to the fasts and prayers of the church. She expressed her willingness to be a part of our church and to participate in prayer activities. As part of her spiritual journey, the young woman took courses for her immersion baptism scheduled for June 2016. Unfortunately, she found a job in another city. For her own self-fulfillment, she was initially engaged to participate in activities within the church's youth ministry.

The follow-up was difficult because she was no longer in the church because of the distance between her city and the church. The only way to remain free after deliverance is to be a disciple of Christ. The disciple must identify with Christ and persevere in faith. We did our duty as God's servant, but unfortunately the baptism did not take place because she found work in another distant city.

Previously, we had planned, after her baptism of water by immersion, to entrust her to the head of the ministry of youth for her involvement. To conclude, I would say that our visit to this young woman in a crisis reflects the expression of the love of Christ. We have fulfilled our pastoral duty about the Word of God (Jn. 5:14). Our purpose was to encourage, strengthen and reassure her that Christ is with her.

5. 2. 3. 2. Case Study #2: Helping someone interested in marriage

Marriage is the first human institution established by God. It is a divine covenant to which the Christian must obey. The concept of marriage is based on Genesis chapiter 2 verses 23 to 24. The bond of marriage is sacred, it unites the man and the woman so that they become one flesh. God wants all men and women to marry and to find a family. But this is not the case today. Many marriages are broken by lack of preparation in prayer and lack of sanctification. We must not ignore that the purpose of marriage is to glorify God.

There are divorces in families because the divine will is not respected; people marry to fill a void in their lives, to satisfy their sexuality, to realize their ambition, or for any kind of unbiblical reason. You do not get married because you should get married. Very often, these people find their marriage relationship by following the following path: Love-marriage - disillusionment - unhappiness - endurance or divorce. This attitude eventually leads to divorce, because it is not the divine will for marriage. This explains why there are so many divorces in the world.

On the other hand, marriage remains one of the most important social institutions in Canada, but the marriage rate is declining and the portrait of the family in the biblical sense of the word is changing. According to Statistics Canada, in 2011, 67% of Canadian families are headed by married couples, compared with 70% in 2001, according to Statistics Canada. In 2011, for the first time in Canadian history, there are more single-person households than couples with children[39]. This shows that the concept of marriage in the biblical sense has lost its value. The Church has a mandate to guarantee and protect this heritage. Biblical counselling must preserve marriage in the church and lead believers to understand what God is expecting from marriage.

In this part of the work, I would like to tell a story that I experienced as a pastor giving importance to biblical counselling. In my church, I am interested in counselling and helping people grow spiritually. It is in this mission that God used me to help a young woman of Catholic background find family stability and appeasement of her sufferings.

---

[39] http://www.encyclopediecanadienne.ca/fr/article/mariage-et-divorce/. Consulted, on 2017-06-05.

Indeed, this woman arrived at our church about two years ago. She came very often in our sessions of fasting and prayer, and to Sunday morning worship. One day, she came to see me, desperate, and asks me for advice because she is much attacked, her life is worth nothing, she is getting old, and she is not yet married.

This became very worrying for her. The fear of the future began to haunt her. I noticed that she was unstable in her life. We exchanged and offered to help her. The program consisted of fervent prayers and pastoral care. We accepted her as a church member so she could benefit from favors according to church rules. That day, she invited a friend to our church and introduced him. I made her understand that the starting point of her deliverance was her acceptance of Jesus as Lord and Savior. She accepted baptism despite her Catholic baptism and her blind attachment to the Catholic Church.

5.2.3.2.1. Baptism by immersion

Biblical courses on baptism began on the following themes: (1) the importance of being baptized; (2) New life and insight into the sacrament. We advanced in the courses of preparation for baptism, until the day that she came to tell me that she wanted to abandon the baptism. We discussed this and I reassured her that Baptism is very important in the counselling, for if you accept Christ then you will accept to be baptized without compromise. She was convinced and agreed to continue. Thus, by the grace of God, her baptism was performed in the church and with the church.

5.2.3.2.2. Find a husband

The young woman and her friend (the one who visited us) came to my office to meet me. The purpose of the meeting was to announce their engagement and seize this opportunity to get married. Glory to God. But a few months later, things remained in uncertainty to such an extent that fear, doubt and anguish continued to settle in her. However, counselling sessions continued in the normal course. We have scheduled several teaching meetings at the Word of God, and pastoral counselling meetings were short-lived, but they were followed and preceded by prayers of authority, for we believe that his situation is special and must be solved in the spiritual realm. I recommended her moments of fasting and prayer that she should manage herself and let God act.

The woman cried to the Lord and God answered her call. The man agreed to take her as his wife and by agreement; they decided that I would celebrate their wedding in church. By the will of God, the marriage took place and God blessed them with a baby to strengthen their marriage. Marriage is a divine institution and God has approved this union. Counselling is a process that depends on the will of the Holy Spirit and the disposition of those involved. Those in search of the divine solution must be reassured.

5. 2. 3. 3. Case Study #3: Helping someone with a divorce problem

We studied in the previous section, commentary to help a Christian who would like to marry. In this part, I would like to discuss a case of divorce; I took part as a Christian counselor. One day, a young married woman came to my church to ask me for spiritual help. She wanted to leave her husband for reasons of incompatibility. This situation ultimately led to divorce. I had several interviews with them individually. The genesis of their first love relationship goes back to their native country. Their new life in Canada, a challenging country for immigrants, has contributed to the conditions leading to their divorce.

In the counselling, the woman told me that her husband did not take care of her properly, that she could not live with him if this attitude persisted. The husband, for his part, said that his wife did not remain so, and their sex lives had changed since their arrival in Canada. I had several interviews with the couple, but with each of the person separately.

I used the Word of God to confront them. I prayed continually for them, and I recommended them to pray and think about their divorce plan while letting them know that God does not grant divorce petitions. After several weeks, I found in counselling that the real problem was not the difficulties evoked by each person. Perhaps they wanted to make a new life together in Canada because they were incompatible in their home country. Life in Canada was a challenge. The African marriage context provides greater security for family cohesion, while life in Canada is much more conducive to divorce. Despite great efforts, prayers, and advice conducted, the couple opted for divorce. Being a Christian, this divorce would not have taken place if they have followed the Word of God.

According to Jay Adams, only adultery and desertion can break the marriage. Apart from these exceptions, marriage is for life. The incompatibility, a frequently cited reason for divorce, has no legitimate status before God. Yet the question of compatibility has become so important that it might be wise to ask, from compatibility to marriage. What can this Christian couple do to be compatible?

But the question remains, compatibility is important. Compatibility is important for a marriage. Although some studies show that people of the same economic, social and educational level seem to get along better, such external compatibility is not essential to a good marriage because it is not fundamental. Studies also mention religion as an important factor. Belief is an essential element of compatibility: Christians should marry only in the Lord and avoid any cause of divorce. Christians should consider biblical counselling as a necessary therapy for the couple living in the covenant of God.

5. 2. 3. 4. Case Study # 4: Helping a couple with an adultery and infertility trouble

Christian couples in difficulty came to me for spiritual help after a few years of pastoral ministry. Their choice seemed appropriate. They knew that the pastor would value healthy family life and stable marriages in accordance with the Bible. Some couples came from other churches, being reluctant to reveal their inner weakness, inadequacies or unfaithfulness to their own pastors. Whatever the reason, Christian couples in difficulty considered me as a biblical advisor. I responded eagerly to the call for help. However, I quickly discovered that my approach to pastoral counselling should be richly intertwined with Scripture, exhortation, encouragement and prayer. The identities and circumstances of the persons referred to in this study have been modified to protect confidentiality. Anna and Pablo are fictitious names.

Pablo is an evangelical Christian, and has been attending our assembly since his arrival in the country. Anna is a Catholic Christian in her thirties. She has been married to Pablo for about ten years. Anna was unemployed and living at Pablo's expense. He wanted to have a better life with his family so he paid for all the immigration procedures to come and live in Canada with his little family.

5.2.3.4.1. Request for pastoral assistance

In March 2019, as the senior pastor of the evangelical church, I received a phone call from this Christian immigrant, Pablo. He wanted to talk to me about his relationship problems. We prayed and then he started to briefly explain his relationship problem to me without going into detail. He warned me that his wife left home after suspecting her of having an extramarital relationship with a friend, following her frequent visits. This friend is married and the two couples are very close friends. He was completely devastated and in shock.

I encouraged him to stay strong and offered to meet them separately and together, afterwards to help them through biblical counselling sessions. I asked to meet his wife alone for about forty-five minutes before coming back to him in another session on another day. I called Anna and offered her a meeting at my office in the church, but she preferred that the consultation be at her friend's house. So I respected her choice and two days later, I went to the appointment.

5.2.3.4.2. Pastoral interview with Anna

I met Anna in order to listen to her and offer her my help even though I am not her pastor. We prayed together and she told me her side of the story. She says that the facts for which she blames her husband go back a long time. Indeed, Pablo had extramarital relations with a young woman. This relationship had caused tensions in their relationship because she had suffered so much, shocked and ridiculed them. Pablo made her believe it was an isolated incident. Pablo and his family immigrated to Canada, Anna notices that her husband has not changed his behaviour in his relationship with this young woman.

She discovered that they call each other on the phone and communicate through social networks. She also mentions that Pablo is not fulfilling his marriage commitment because she discovered in his cell phone notes of love and pornographic photos of the young woman. She currently holds physical evidence from her mobile phone. She also mentions that

Pablo accuses her of having an extramarital relationship with the neighbour's husband of whom they are close friends. Anna also refuses to break off friendly relations with this couple. However, Anna acknowledges her deep friendship with the other couple and rejects any suspicion of adultery that might implicate her. We ended the meeting with a prayer. I proposed another counselling session at the church. I asked her to contact me to continue the accompaniment session.

5.2.3.4.3. Pastoral interview with Pablo

Almost a year after arriving in Canada, Pablo had a stroke while driving his vehicle. What is a stroke? It is a sudden loss of brain function caused by a loss of blood flow in the brain. Following this accident, he was hospitalized in the hospital for several weeks. As a pastor, he confided in me about his adulterous relationship with another woman before he arrived in Canada and he also received threats of divorce from his wife.

Indeed, when Pablo was on his hospital bed, his girlfriend texted him to know how his health was. She told him that despite the distance between them, she still loves him. Pablo also replied that he loved her and let her know that since he came to this country, he is facing many bad circumstances. To comfort him from his illness, she sent him by SMS (short message service) photos in which she shows off her body outdoors. Anna was sitting on the hospital bed and took advantage of a moment of inattention to spy on Pablo and monitor his suspicious behavior with her cell phone.

Despite the password's complexity, she was able to remember this code and then unlock the mobile phone while Pablo slept on the hospital bed. She discovered the imaginable: notes of love, unhealthy unpublished photos from the other woman.

She quickly transferred all this information to her own cell phone. The drop of water had just broken the camel's back. The legitimate woman blamed her husband for his unhealthy behaviour and the intimate relationship he has with her from their country of origin. The man told her not to focus on this case right now, but that they should focus together on his illness situation because there is no longer an extramarital relationship between him and this woman since they came to Canada. Pablo lets his wife know that he needs her affection and presence with him in these difficult times in his life.

The man thought this story was closed. After a long stay in hospital, he emerges with sequelae that reduce his motor skills (Inertia of an arm, asymmetry of the face). This handicap does not allow him to work with ease. He will enter another phase of his life. The new life will be difficult with his wife who, according to him, refuses to obey him, to love him in suffering. She starts to disrespect him, she frequents too much a neighbouring couple whose friendship has deteriorated between him and the other man. He suspects that he covets his wife: he suspects that his wife is cheating on him with this man. He repeats to his spouse and complains to her when she spends a lot of time with the couple in question.

Pablo does not understand the situation in which he lives. Things have changed at home and his wife is not very respectful. In addition, Pablo reveals that since his discharge from the hospital, sexual relations with his wife have taken place at intervals of once a month because there are times when she refuses to have sex with him.

During the preliminaries of sexual intercourse, Anna is indifferent and does not take part. Sexual foreplay is a truly delightful time of sensual exchange and growing excitement. Anna makes her husband believe that she is tired of having sex with him, that she doesn't think about it, that he has to stay quiet because he is sick. Pablo thinks Anna has extramarital intimate relationships. Pablo also blames his wife for spending too much time with her friend's husband, an attitude that cannot be tolerated in a respectable couple.

Pablo has no idea if the couple's married wife knows anything about her husband's love affairs and behaviour towards his own wife. Pablo points out to his wife that this man is disrespectful to her and Anna finds that Pablo exaggerates a little and calls him a hypocrite. Pablo replies by calling his wife ungrateful, ungrateful woman for the benefits.

The couple entered into an endless argument. During their dispute, several old problems arose. It's time for the score-settling. Pablo is no longer working, the financial needs are there. He points out that before his accident, he still has to pay the rent and take care of the family. As for his wife, since she has been working, her salary has been saved at the bank and she uses the government family allowances paid to her for the benefit of the child to pay bills and grocery shopping for the house. Pablo is discouraged and regrets marrying her and bringing her to Canada as a landed immigrant.

Anna threatens to leave the family home and move in alone. The arguments have resumed intensely. Despite his disability, Pablo tried to get a small part-time job to support himself. One morning, he had gone to work, when he returned from work, he noticed that his wife was absent. Worried, he tries to reach her on his mobile phone, but no answer. The next day, he managed to talk to her and she informed him that she did not want to go home for the time being. Anna had taken her things to stay in a place unknown to her husband. Seeking help, Pablo came into contact with her family and friends, including her pastor, but Anna remained unchanged about her decision.

5.2.3.4.4. Pastoral encouragement and exhortation

This session was with Pablo who accepted that his pastor exhorted him and guided him through the Word of God. We studied Galatians 5 from verse 16. The purpose of this exhortation is to let him know that we must not abuse Christian freedom. In verse 16, the apostle Paul shows us that Christians can avoid fulfilling the desires of the flesh if they walk by the Spirit, for the flesh has desires contrary to those of the Spirit and the Spirit has desires contrary to those of the flesh. Pablo realized that these two things are opposed to each other. If he and Anna walk in the Spirit, they will not do the things they want. I confronted Pablo with the Scriptures by showing him that his home is currently under the law because they are not led by the Spirit (v. 18).

They must understand that as long as he and his wife are led by fornication, uncleanness, dissolution, idolatry, quarrels, jealousies, animosities, disputes, divisions, desires, debaucheries and the like, they will be under the wrath of God and will not inherit the kingdom of God (v. 19). I mentioned to Pablo that he has sinned against God alone and to regain his communion with Him, it will take a true prayer of repentance (Ps. 51:3-6), that is, confessing his sins (fornication, impurity, quarrels, jealousy, disputes, divisions, envy, drunkenness, debauchery). He will also have to ask God for forgiveness (Ps. 51) and then turn away from these sins, that is, not to return to them again.

The couple must understand that repentance is the act of expressing grief for something bad they have done. On the scriptural level, it is a change that occurs in the mind and heart, that permeates the soul and mind and leads to changes in external actions and spiritual direction. Repentance is not only an emotional response. It is a decision, a resolution that is both important and necessary to avoid spiritual death (Lk. 13:3).

The members of the couple, must repent regularly. The Bible constantly gives examples related to repentance: believers in Corinth were mandated to repent (2 Corinthians 7:9), Ephesians were led to repentance (Rev. 2:5) and believers in Pergamos, Sardis and Laodicea were called to repentance (Rev. 2:16; 3:3; 3:19). People are drawn to repentance by the goodness of God (Rom. 2:4). In addition, Pablo and Anna must stand firm in freedom in Christ, and guard against seducers prowling around them. He understood that these sins gave legal access to the enemy in his life. Under my direction, Pablo read Psalm 51, and followed the steps to regain his communion with God. The following Sunday, he came to the church and we prayed for him. A week later, I sent a message to Anna to follow up on her relationship difficulties. Four days after I spoke with Anna, Pablo informed me that she had returned home.

5.2.3.4.5. How can a man cope with sexual infidelity

Pablo admitted that before he arrived in the country, he had already had sexual relations with a woman other than his lawful spouse. This is what the Bible calls adultery (2S. 11:2-4). Adultery is a sin and a flagrant violation of the marriage covenant. The authentic Christian must not commit adultery (De. 5:18). The Bible strongly condemns sexual infidelity (Lv. 18:20). Adultery always has unfortunate consequences on the home and can lead to situations such as broken homes, unwanted pregnancies (2Sa. 11.5), sexually transmitted diseases and negative emotions such as guilt, fear, shame and anxiety.

According to our approach to the biblical helping relationship, we urged Pablo to face adultery: Pablo should no longer feed his thoughts with fantasies. He must reject impure thoughts because the desire to covet a woman is considered adultery. Jesus teaches us that the simple desire to have sex with a woman other than your lawful spouse is already an adultery in thought, and therefore a sin. Intention is worth the act (Mt. 5:27-28). As long as Pablo is in contact with this young woman, he will always remain in sin and hold pornographic photos of her. Since his arrival in Canada, Pablo has been faithful to his spouse with his body, but not with his mind, thus breaking the trust necessary for the solidity of the marriage and putting himself in a position of infidelity. He must learn to control his thoughts because bad thoughts inspire bad deeds. It is very important to remember that the seductive words of unfaithful women constitute a formidable trap where the one whom the Lord disapproves of falls (Pr. 22:14).

We led Pablo to confess adultery as a sin that God hates. The Bible teaches that "He who hides his sins does not prosper, but he who confesses and renounces them finds mercy" (Pr. 28:13). Pablo naturally tends to hide his mistakes. The biblical principle of repentance is that we must first openly acknowledge our mistakes and sins and then ask forgiveness, analyze the situation and correct what is needed to prevent it from happening again.

- We also advised Pablo to break off unhealthy relationships with his adulterous partner. This act is condemned several times in the Bible. We warned him not to communicate with her in any way. The apostle Paul writes (2 Co. 6:17-18):

"Come out of them and be separated, says the Lord. Touch nothing unclean, and I will receive you."

God calls his children not to associate with unbelievers in order not to sin against him. Christians should not sinned, he has done what is wrong in his eyes (Ps. 51:4-6). We advised Pablo to rely on David's prayer (Ps. 51) to pray to God. We must finally remember that God condemns marital infidelity and all forms of conjugal infidelity.

5.2.3.4.6. Comments and biblical view of the situation

When we look at the reactions of the Pablo and Anna couple, we can deduce that these Christians are not exemplary in their behavior and in the way they solve their problem. The fact that Pablo and Anna are not of the same Christian denomination complicates the resolution of the conflict a little. Pablo, from an evangelical background, seems to give importance to the words of her Pastor and the Bible, while Anna, from a Catholic background, does not see things in the same way.

There is a lot to talk about this couple. We certainly observe that there is marital infidelity and communication problems in the couple. The real source of the problem is due to the fact that the couple is physiologically unable to conceive a baby naturally. Anna's infertility situation is proving unbearable for her couple. This situation, which has been going on for more than five years, has probably led Pablo to choose an option by having sex outside marriage with this adulterous partner.

The scientific literature (Squires et al., 2008), reports that there are cases of infertility that are medically unexplained. In addition, researchers have shown that in unexplained infertility, minor deficits exist in both members of the couple, potentiate and conjugate, while with another partner a pregnancy could occur. The psychological dimension of infertility is rarely questioned (Bydlowski, 2004). Similarly, the spiritual dimension is often ignored.

have unhealthy relationships with non-believers. The Old Testament warns God's children of the dangers of being united with unbelieving women. The King's book tells us here the evidence (1 Ki. 11:4-8):

King Solomon loved many foreign women besides Pharaoh's daughter: Moabites, Ammonites, Edomites, Sidonians, Hittites, belonging to the nations whose Lord had said to the children of Israel: You shall not go to them, nor shall they come to you; they shall certainly turn your hearts to their gods. It was to these nations that Solomon, driven by love, became attached. He had seven hundred princesses for wives and three hundred concubines; and his wives turned his heart away.

In Solomon's old age, his wives inclined his heart to other gods; and his heart was not complete to the Lord his God, as had been the heart of David his father.

Solomon went after Astarte, the god of the Sidonians, and after Milcom, the abomination of the Ammonites; and Solomon did that which was evil in the sight of the Lord, and did not fully follow the Lord, as David his father did.

Through Solomon's story, God warns us that loving relationships or interested associates with foreign or pagan women should be perceived as a threat to the integrity of the faith. The reason is simple because they can turn Christians away from the true God.

- We got Pablo to apologize to Anna, his lawful wife and girlfriend, who he is hurting.

- We urged Pablo to ask God to restore his marriage, to cleanse him completely of his iniquity, and to purify him of his sin. Pablo acknowledges his transgressions, and his sin is constantly before him. It is against God alone that he has

In our approach to the biblical counselling, the spiritual dimension is very important to understand what is really happening in this couple. If we consider the spiritual dimension in this situation, we can discern that Anna's infertility reveals the spiritual realm. Any spiritual problem must be solved spiritually. Anna is blowing evil influence that would prevent her from conceiving a baby with Pablo. According to our analysis and with discernment, this infertility problem would not come from Pablo because he has a big boy who was born before he was in a relationship with Anna. Medicine has failed in its treatment of Anna's infertility. Where science fails, it is where God acts and succeeds. Nothing is impossible for God because he is sovereign and his sovereignty lasts forever. The Bible tells of many healings of infertility. In Jewish Old Testament thought, for the first 10 years after marriage, a woman without children was considered a barren woman. This was a valid reason for divorce and remarriage in favour of the man.

Anna should put her hope in God because Jesus has not changed in his goodness and willingness to heal his children. The Bible mentions the names of several women who have become fertile: the story of Sarah, wife of Abraham, and mother of Isaac (Gn. 21), Rebecca, wife of Isaac, who will give birth to the twins Esau and Jacob (Gn. 25); Rachel, wife of Jacob, and mother of Joseph (Gn. 30); Samson was born of a barren mother (Jg. 13), Anne, mother of Samuel (1 Sa. 2); Elizabeth, mother of John the Baptist (Lk. 1).

Our analysis allows us to conclude that Anna's infertility led her to feel inadequate as a wife, and to lose hope for future happiness. She must understand that God is sovereign, therefore, she must cede all her rights to God and he will meet her needs. A word from the prophet Jeremiah that confirms our opinions (Jr. 29:11):

"For I know the thoughts that I think toward you, saith the LORD, thoughts of peace, and not of evil, to give you an expected end."

She must know that God can make her fertile:

"Jacob made love to Rachel also, and his love for Rachel was greater than his love for Leah. And he worked for Laban another seven years" (Gn. 29:30)

"And God remembered Rachel, and God hearkened to her, and opened her womb."(Gn. 30:22)

Anna must trust God, she must have a frank and sincere relationship with her husband, this is the foundation of marriage (Gn. 2:24):

"Therefore, shall a man leave his father and his mother, and shall cleave unto his wife: and they shall be one flesh."

5. 2. 3. 5. Case Study # 5: Conflict with idolatry, infidelity and immorality

This session deals with a case of conflict between idolatry, infidelity and immorality in a local church. This is the story of an apparently "Christian" couple who are seeking positions as elders and deacons in a local church. Unfortunately, the Pastor's interview with this couple reveals that this family leads a double life (syncretism: the combination of different forms of belief or practice). This story is real and is found in many churches around the world. It can exist, elect domicile and live in your assembly. To preserve the identity of individuals, the real names of the people have been changed. As part of our work in this area, we had to meet with a pastor to discuss with him his experiences in the field of biblical counselling in his church.

Thus, this Pastor Teacher had the opportunity to share with one of his many cases of christian counselling lived and resolved according to the word of God in some of his churches in Canada, Africa and America. In the light of the Holy Scriptures, we will attempt to interpret these behaviours, analyses and especially the approaches used by the Pastor in resolving his many conflicts in order to propose a possible dialectic, if necessary theological and biblical solutions.

5.2.3.5.1. The history of the facts (event)

The event goes back several years. In his plan to establish leadership in his Church, the pastor, with the agreement of his council of elders of his congregation, the initiative was taken by the Pastor to ordain or raise a couple from his church to the rank of elders and deaconess. This family is a member in good standing of the church and participates effectively and actively in all church ceremonies. Apparently, the couple is biblically flawless. The pastor's plan to consecrate this legitimate brother and sister in the Lord was based on the apostle Paul's recommendations to Timothy on the qualifications of bishops in the church and on how to lead God's church. According to the apostle Paul, if a person aspires to the office of deacon: This person must be honest, far from duplicity, from the excesses of wine, from a sordid gain, he must be tested first, and before exercising his ministry afterwards, if he is a blameless person". The apostle also extends this recommendation to women (1 Tim 3:8-15):

> "And withal they learn to be idle, wandering about from house to house; and not only idle, but tattlers also and busybodies, speaking things which they ought not. I will therefore that the

younger women marry, bear children, guide the house, give none occasion to the adversary to speak reproachfully. For some are already turned aside after Satan."

During their meeting the pastor reminded the couple of Paul's recommendations. The purpose of the pastor's interview with the couple was to verify and confirm qualifications for the exercise of an authoritative function in the church. The Pastor reminded them of the prerequisites, according to Paul, for running the house of God. He asked them about their intimate relationship with God. The Bible reveals that our words and actions must reflect our faith in God. In other words: "It is from the abundance of the heart that the mouth speaks (Lk. 6:45)".

The woman taking the Pastor aside, in another individual meeting, answers the pastor that she is currently in separation from her husband even though they live in the same house. She still makes revelations to the pastor saying that she has fetishes in her luggage protecting her parents and grandparents. The pastor advised the woman to hand over the fetishes to him to burn them. He suggested that he pray with the couple in accordance with Paul's letters to Timothy and Titus concerning the qualification (1 Tm. 3:1, Tt. 1:5-10). To the pastor's question to the family: "Who is protecting you now, your fetishes or God? Their answer is unequivocal.

Our analysis of the situation and solution approach according to the Scriptures.

In this pastor's story, this Christian couple had a lot to blame themselves for. He is going through difficult times in their homes despite their hypocrisy in the Lord's work. Their hypocrisy in their commitment to God greatly opens the doors to the enemy in their lives. The Bible warns us that the devil prowls around Christians to bring them down (1P. 5:8). The couple downgraded, in example both partners gradually moved away from their Christian commitment. Although they are present in the church for activities, their spirit is in the world (spiritual death). They no longer have an intimate relationship with God. They hid their transgression in front of the church by remaining in hypocrisy. We need to understand why this happened in this couple. This couple is Canadian but of African origin so they immigrated to Canada to have a better social life. However, we are of the opinion that most immigrants, especially of African origin, have a great socio-professional challenge to face and that it is not obvious to serve God in this context.

This factor would contribute to the relaxation of the faith of immigrant Christians because they are caught between two worlds, that of God (in the church) and that of the secular. Another important factor to consider is the phenomenon of acculturation (change in the original culture). Many people call themselves Christians but live in sin continuously without repentance and without the fear of God. The sin of infidelity is an old and serious problem that threatens churches. This transgression crosses the entire Bible, including King David's adulterous sin, the fall of his son King Solomon, the problems concerning the Church of the Corinthians, the many recommendations on this subject in Paul's epistles (Ro.13:8,7:1-3).

In our case study, the spouse committed a sin of adultery (Ga. 5:16) because he probably lacks sexual satisfaction with his wife, who is very concerned about societal challenges (protection, success or social success). This explains her confidence in fetishisms when she resorted to the forces of darkness. God does not share His worship with other gods.

In this couple, mutual trust is no longer up to date, even in God. This atmosphere weakens family cohesion.

As far as the pastor's intervention is concerned, the approach is legitimate and biblical, but his approach of counselling remains insufficient because the couple left the church and subsequently the divorce was pronounced. The purpose of a biblical counselling is to bring back souls who have moved away from God while creating the conditions for spiritual accompaniment. It is a process that goes beyond a simple encounter with biblical verses. The roots of the problem must be exposed. Adultery and idolatry are only the manifestations of sin. Their problem is spiritual and therefore the remedy must be spiritual in nature. Paul advises us to walk in the Spirit and we will not fulfill the desires of the flesh (Ro. 5:6).

On the spiritual level, the couple is sick and needs faith therapy that cannot be possible through the power of the Holy Spirit.

The role of the pastor should be oriented towards practical work that encourages the couple in counselling to rethink their way of seeing problems and to follow an enlightened direction. The pastor is subject to the authority of the Holy Scriptures. He should seek to analyze the problems of the couple from the point of view of the Word of God. It should encourage the couple to reflect on all aspects of their lives based on the Word of God. The couple needs to be transformed by the renewal of their minds and to address difficulties according to God's thought.

5. 2. 3. 6. Case Study #6: Depression: Painful experience of an inconsolable woman

As part of the practical exercises related to Bible counselling and its application in the local church, I met a pastor who told me about his experience with an inconsolable woman.

This story will serve as a model for a practical exercise related to the steps of biblical counselling. The purpose of the exercise is not to evaluate the pastoral approach but rather to put into practice the steps of the biblical counselling based on a real and lived story. Here is the historicity as reported by the pastor: "This testimony is a painful experience lived by a woman in her relationship life. She came into my office in tears.

Here's what she said to me : "I am here to ask for your help, Pastor. I'm a widow, my husband is dead. His death caused me a depression. One time I was coming back from work and I found my husband in the kitchen cooking. My husband gave me a kiss. We were both happy. While they were at the table eating, my husband's cell phone rang. It was a woman saying good night to him. I got angry with my husband right after that message. I went to the room. I was sulking. My husband looked at me and said to himself inside:" "You are not nice, my wife. For a simple message you get angry? I am not going to follow you."

The husband ends up having dinner without me. He came to sleep in bed. But we weren't talking to each other. Back to back, no words all night long. Around midnight, my husband was laying his hand on me, I refused to let him touch me. But I realized he was sweating. I didn't go back, the woman said to see why her husband was sweating like that. The husband didn't look like him, so he ended up dying of a stroke. In the morning, the woman gets up, dresses, eats breakfast and goes to work. When the woman returns from work in the afternoon, she finds a beautiful watch she bought to calm her husband's anger. She enters the house, she finds that her husband's breakfast was not consumed. She hurries to go to the room. She finds her husband in the same position as she left him in the morning. She felt that her husband was no longer alive. But she thought, her husband will come to talk to her himself first. However, the husband had already been dead since midnight. A painful observation seized her and she cried, she cried. She was inconsolable. After she had given me her testimony, I prayed and started counselling her."

5.2.3.6.1. Commentary and the scriptural Answer

What comment could we make here? The most important thing for us in this study is the lived history of the woman. We see that this widow's life was increasingly dominated by anxiety and then depression. In his meeting with the pastor. She feels guilty and constantly anxious about whether her attitude contributed to her spouse's accident. She seems inconsolable and comes to confide in the pastor to receive comfort and prayer. We will see how practical exercises can end her distress and help this woman to trust God.

From the first meeting, with careful listening, the counsellor should collect information about the woman (see Appendix A) that will help to better understand the contexts of her marital life and offer her adapted exercises to get to the heart of her attitude (depression and anxiety). She is in an emotional state characterized by feelings of continued despair, inadequacy, gloom, sadness and difficulty thinking, concentrating and acting. She lives in despair and eventually has suicidal thoughts. The death of her spouse and her guilt are two negative circumstances or factors that triggered depression and anxiety.

Bible verses are true supports to guide Christians in their daily personal lives. Therefore, it is important to highlight depression and anxiety and to confront this woman with biblical promises. Psalm 121 is an opportunity to enter the universe of these fears and build a biblical helping relationship with her. For this reason, we would recommend several readings of Psalm 121 during the week after the first meeting with the counsellor. The Word of God says (Ps. 121):

> "I look up to the mountains. Where will the help come from? Help comes to me from the Lord, Who made heaven and earth. He will not allow but your foot to wobble; he who keeps you will not slumber. Behold, he neither slumbers nor sleeps, He who keeps Israel. The Lord is your keeper, the Lord is your shadow in your right hand. In the daytime the sun will not strike you, Nor the moon in the night. The Lord will keep you from all evil, He will keep your soul; The Lord will keep your departure and your arrival, from now on and for ever".

Psalm 121 presents the Lord Jesus as a protector who helps people in distress or depression when a call for help is asked. In this psalm the faithful turns his eyes away from the reality of his affliction and lifts his eyes to the Lord who is the creator of the mountains. God responds to the trust of the faithful with personal and reassuring promises (Ps. 121:3-8).

The meditation of this psalm should draw the attention of the anguished and depressed woman to three facts: The God of the Bible holds absolute control over all creation. It has the power to neutralize everything that is harmful, including the situation in which we are currently living. God watches over his people and over every believer. With this first meeting, other meetings should be scheduled in the same model as the first (Biblical Promises). The practical exercises with Bible verses involving this woman serve to remove her barriers of anxiety and depression so that she can develop an intimate relationship with God.

To conclude the approach used to accompany a depressed person could be summarized as follows: the Bible counselor should identify the root cause. How did his state of depression begin? When did it start? What is the main cause? Are negative emotions the cause of things like anger and non-pardon or guilt? saying that she has fetishes in her luggage protecting her parents and grandparents.

The goal of all biblical counseling is to help the troubled person reprogram his or her mind through the power of God's Word by immersing him or herself in it. The Word of God can transform all aspects of one's life physically, mentally, emotionally and spiritually. Here is what the Bible says in Philippians 4:6-7:

"Do not be anxious about anything, but in everything present your requests to God with prayers and supplications, with thanksgiving. And the peace of God, which surpasses all understanding, will guard your hearts and minds in Christ Jesus."

This inconsolable woman has reason to worry at home, the advice the Bible gives is to turn her worries into prayers and pray without ceasing. Only the certainty of God's sovereignty can bring her true peace, which is not that of the world. As a Christian, her membership in the Kingdom of God is assured, her destiny is fixed and she can have victory over her worries. Prayer and the Word of God are two powerful tools to ward off adversity and reclaim the blessings stolen by the enemy. They allow one to focus on God alone rather than on one's problems, and to recognize that God's ultimate goal is to do good. For God knows the plans he has for his children; they are plans for peace and not for evil (Jer. 29:11).

CHAPITER VI:

DISCUSSION AND PERSONNAL VIEWPOINT

As we have already seen above, in general, there are two types of counselling, the secular counselling and the Christian counselling. It emerges from our analysis that the two concepts of counselling have different approaches. The first is to provide temporary therapy while the second leads to a change of attitude, an inner transformation of the counselee. The Bible remains the legitimate standard for godly counselling. The Bible is better placed to teach the actions of Jesus from a counselling perspective.

The Christian counselling approach considers the interpretation of the biblical text to accompany the counsellee. For the difficulties of man, the biblical text offers solutions. The Holy Scriptures should be used for pastoral counselling. Jesus' interview with characters such as Nicodemus, Zacchaeus, the Samaritan woman and the adulterous woman, allows us to understand the basic principles of biblical counselling. We also noticed that Jesus' way of acting and doing positively influenced his interview with these characters.

Starting from the pedagogy of Christ, it is of paramount importance that Christian counsellors in our churches should truly be called by God and have a solid biblical training and a spirit of prayer. Since the exercise of this ministry requires in-depth knowledge of the Word of God. Also, Jay Adams did not hesitate to emphasize that "prayer is the basis of all biblical counselling."

In secular counselling, it is the theories that are applied for temporary therapy. In Christian counselling, it is through prayer that the Holy Spirit transforms the hearts of those suffering. It is important to note that in today's counselling, each case of a counsellors should relate directly or indirectly to a biblical counselling situation. So, there is always a biblical solution to any problem, because nothing is impossible with God. The Christian counsellors should imitate Jesus Christ in his counselling approach which is valid throughout all the time.

CONCLUSION

We have come to the apotheosis that there is a clear difference between secular counselling and biblical counselling. For, indeed, in biblical counselling, the Word of God is the standard of every situation, thus demanding a strictly spiritual relationship. It is also established that the Jesus-centered ministry of counselling demands a great deal of availability and challenges from both a human and a spiritual point of view.

Nevertheless, it is permissible for us to observe in the canonical Gospels that Jesus did not trust only to those who were suffering or in search of consolation. But He was always focused on their spiritual problem. Thus, the Apostle John always seem to show through his Gospel that the conversation of Jesus with Nicodemus was spiritual. Hence the absolute necessity for a spiritual counsellors to be totally endowed with divine authority. That is why Jesus gives all authority to the Christians called to exercise this kind of ministry when he says, *"Behold, I have given you power to walk on the serpents and scorpions, and over all the power of the enemy; And nothing will harm you*[40]*"*. Human sciences such as contemporary psychology with all its derivatives cannot bring about the cure of the soul nor console man in disarray. It is the Holy Spirit who is the great Comforter[41].

[40] Lk. 10. 19
[41] Jn. 15. 26

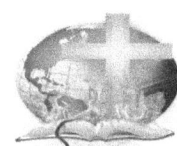

From the Desk of
Rev. Dr. Terrance Jenkins, Th. D., Ph. D.

I met Dr. Atche several years ago while speaking at a conference in Quebec but then a few years later we became well acquainted as he made contact concerning extra theological and counseling training at our school in Montreal—Montreal School of Ministry. Since that time, I have had the privilege of working with him to gain the Master of Christian Counselling and Doctorate of Theology degrees.

When Dr. Atche asked if I would write something for him about his new project I was pleased to say "yes" without hesitation because I have come to know his heart for God and for helping people. He is a man of God, teacher, pastor avid student of the Word, quite astute concerning what troubles people, and more. The hypothesis put forth for his work entitled "The Divine Way to Help CHRISTIANS in Troubled Times" based on biblical counseling approaches is timely and deserves to be read by all who are in any ministry position and planning to enter any ministry office.

This man of God does not profess to have all of the answers for all of the needs of humanity through secular or Christian counseling but he does serve the One who does have the answers—Jesus Christ.

In this work, Rev. Brou points out certain aspects of the secular in contrast with the whole of Christian counselling to bring out the correct principles to use in helping those who are in distress to bring about godly change in the person's life.

He shows how attitude determines altitude; how a change in thinking brings about a change in behavior; and how the Holy Spirit is the One who give guidance in all counselling situations, without Whose guidance there could be no effective biblical (Christian) counselling.

He shows that counselling is not Christian just because a Christian is doing the counselling or using the Bible. Counselling can only be called Christian when it points the counsellee to the Great Counselor - the Lord Jesus Christ.

The author puts forth several case studies for illustration purposes but does not claim that his work is comprehensive or exhaustive enough to cover all areas of counseling. Nonetheless, the principles put forth in this work will give the investigative counsellor enough information to get him/her a foundation for biblical counselling.

This work is a must read for future godly counsellors.

APPENDIX A: PERSONAL DATA INVENTORY

DATA INVENTORY[42],[43]

A-1. Identification Data

Name ....

Phone..

Address..

Occupation ....

Birth date ....

Civil Status: () Single   () Maried

            () Divorced   () Going Steady

            () Cohabitant   () Widowed

Your job

Your age

Name and surname of the person who sent you to us ....

....

....

....

---

[42] Paul MILLEMAN, *La relation d'aide, vocation de l'Église.* France, Éditions Excelsis, 2014. p.465-474.

[43] Adams JAY, The Christian Counselor's Manual: The Practice of Nouthetic Counselling, Grand Rapids, Michigan, Zondervan Publishing House, 1986, p.436

What primary education did you receive and what secondary and higher levels did you do? (Also mention the evening classes and the apprenticeship you may have followed.)

....

....

....

....

A-2. Health information

What is your general state?

() Excellent   () Good

() not very good   () Declining

Last time:

() You've gained weight,

() You've lost weight

() Your weight has not changed

Name the illnesses, injuries, disabilities and significant operations you have or have suffered:

....

....

....

....

Have you ever used "soft medicine" (acupuncture, homeopathy, etc.)?

....

....

....

Do you currently take any medications?

() Yes   () No

Which?

....

Do you suffer from insomnia?

() Yes   () No

How many stops due to illness have you had in the past 12 months?

....

Do you agree that your advisor will share information about your medical condition, social status, and spiritual condition with your general practitioner?

() Yes   () No

With an elder from your local church?

() Yes   () No

Check the symptoms that apply to you?

() Skin disorder   () Migraine   () Disorders of balance
() Urinary disorder() Decreased appetite () Constipation
() Vertigo   () Palpitations   ()Memory loss(amnesia)
() Asthma   () Stomach pain   () Sleep interrupted
() Back pain   () Digestive disorders () Sleep Disorder
() Concentration   () Loss/Weight Increase.
() Decreased/increased sexual appetite

A-3. Religious background

Denominational preference: ....

Member since: ....

Church Attendance per month (circle) 0 1 2 3 4 5 6 7 8 9 10 +

Church attended in childhood: ....
Baptized? Yes.....No.....

Religious background of your spouse (if married)................

Do you believe in God? Yes......No........Uncertain...................

Do you pray to God? Never....Occasionally....Often................

Are you saved? Yes......No.......Not sure what you mean...........

Do you have regular family devotion? Yes........No........

Explain recent changes in your religious life, if any

Let us suppose that this night you would die and God ask you; "Why would I get you into heaven? What would you say?"

....

....

Do you read the Bible?
() Never   () Sometimes   () Often

Do you worship with your family?
()Never   () Sometimes   () Often

Do you have a responsibility in your church?......................

....

Have there been changes in your spiritual life lately? ....

....

A-4. Personality information

Do you have any personal problems?
Yes..........No............

Describe them: ....

Have you ever had any psychotherapy or counselling before?

Yes........No.........

If yes, list counselors or therapist and dates:

....

....

What was the outcome?

....

....

Have you ever taken any drugs, or alcoholic beverages for a non-medical purpose?

Yes.............No.................If so, what did you take ....

Have you been arrested?   Yes.............No.................

If so, why? ....

Quote at least three quality which a friend appreciates (estimates) in you ....

....

Quote at least three defects that people complain about ....

....

What is the purpose of your life:

....

....

....

Which are you favourite pasttimes: ....

....

....

....

....

Circle any of the following words which best describe you now:

() Active   () Ambitious   () Self-confident
() Persistent   () Nervous   () Hardworking
() Impatient   () Impulsive   () Moody
() Often-blue   () Excitable   () Imaginative
() Calm   () Serious   () Easy-going
() Shy   () Good-natured   () Introvert
() Extrovert   () Likeable   () Leader
() Quiet   () Hard-boiled   () Submissive
() Lonely   ()Self-concious   () Sensitive

() Other:..
....

A-5. Marriage and family information

Name of spouse: ....
Address: ....
....
Phone: ....
Occupation: ....
Business phone: ....
Your spouse's age:..........Education (in years)...........
Religion..........
Date of marriage: ....
Your ages when married:

Husband:..................................Wife:................................

How long did you know your spouse before marriage?
....
Length of steady dating with spouse ....
Length of engagement...
How did you get to know your spouse?
....
....
....
....

Have you ever been separated? Yes:........No:.........When
from:.......to:..

Has either of you ever filed for divorced? Yes.....No........
When...........

Check of the points that make trouble in your conjugal life.

() Use of household money   () Friends
() Leisure   () Leisure use and organization
() In-laws   () Child education
() Good manners   () Woman's submission

() Communication   () Affection manifestations
() Sexuality   () Authority of man
() The conception of life

Other points: ....

Is your spouse willing to come for counselling: Yes:...No:....
Uncertain:.....

Information about children:

PM*	Full Name	Age	Sex	Living (yes / no)	Education (in years)	Marital status

* Check this column if child is from a previous marriage
Are your children willing to participate in the interviews?

Name: ....
() Yes   () No   Uncertain
Name: ....
() Yes   () No   Uncertain
Name: ....
() Yes   () No   Uncertain
Name: ....
() Yes   () No   Uncertain
Name: ....
() Yes   () No   Uncertain

Information about the parental family

The father still lives? () Yes   () No   Age:...........

Occupation: ....

Quote at least three traits of characters:

....

....

....

The mother still lives? () Yes   () No   Age: ....
Occupation: ....
Quote at least three traits of its characters...........................

....

....

....

How is the marital life of your parents (relatives)?

() Very good   () Good   () Average   () bad

If you have not been raised by your parents, briefly state why: ....

....

....

....

If you have not been raised by your own parents, briefly state why ....

....

....

How many older brothers......sisters...... do you have?

How many younger brothers... sisters...... do you have?

1 BRIEFLY ANSWER THE FOLLOWING QUESTIONS:

a- What is your problem?

b- What have you done about it?

c- What can we do (What are your expectations in coming here)?

d- As you see yourself, what kind of person are you. Describe yourself.

e- What, if anything, do you fear?

f- Is there any other information we should know?

APPENDIX B: COUNSELLOR'S CHECK LIST

CHECK LIST[44]

1. Determine whether evangelism is indicated.
2. Sort out responsibilities.
3. Gather concrete data.
4. Stress what rather than why for data.
5. Distinguish presentation, performance, and preconditioning problem.
6. Talk not only about problems; talk also about God's solutions.
7. Check motivation (ultimately it must be loving obedience: because God says so.)
8. Insist on obedience to God regardless of how one feels.
9. Check out Agendas.
10. Give concrete homework at every session. (Explain "how to"; begin with single-stranded problems.)
11. Check on homework.
12. Would a medical checkup be advisable?

---

[44] Ibid p.436

APPENDIX C: SCRIPTURES USED IN COUNSELLING

SELECTED SCRIPTURES FOR USE IN COUNSELLING[45]

ANXIETY AND WORRY

Psalms 43:5 ; Matthew 6:31, 32 ; Philippians 4:6, 7; Philippians 4:19; I Peter 5:7

BEREAVEMENT AND LOSS

Deuteronomy 31: 8 ; Psalms 27:10 ; Psalms 119: 50; Psalms 119: 92; 2 Corinthians 6:10; Philippians 3:8.

COMFORT

Psalms 23:4; Lamentations 3:22-23; Matthew 5:4; Matthew 11:28-30; John 14:16, 18; Romans 15:4; 2 Corinthians 1:3, 4; 2 Thessalonians 2:16, 17

CONFIDENCE (developing)

Psalms 27:3 ; Proverbs 3:26 ; Proverbs 14:26; Isaiah 30:15 ; Galatians 6:9; Ephesians 3:11, 12 ; Philippians 4:13 ; Philippians 1:6 ; Hebrews 10:35 ; 1 Peter 2:9

DANGER (Protection from)

Psalms 23:4 ; Psalms 32:7; Psalms 34:7; Psalms 34:17; Psalms 34.19; Psalms 91:1 ; Psalms 91:11; Psalms 121:8 ; Isaiah 43:2 ; Romans 14:8.

[45] Clyde NARRAMORE, *Psychology of Counselling*, Grand Rapids, Michigan, Zondervan Publishing House, 1960, p. 258-259.

DISCOURAGEMENT

Joshua 1: 9; Psalms 2 7. 14; Psalms 43:5 ; John 14:1; John 14:27 ; John 16:33 ; Hebrews 4:16 ; 1 John 5:14.

FAITH

Romans 4: 3; Romans 10:17; Ephesians 2:8, 9; Hebrews 11:1; Hebrews 1:6 ; Hebrews 12: 2; James 1:3; James 1:5, 6;1 Peter 1:7.

DEATH

Psalms 23:4 ; Psalms 116:15 ; Lamentations 3:32, 33 ; Romans 14:8 ; 2 Corinthians 5:1 ; Philippians 1:21 ; 1 Thessalonians 5:9-10 ; Hebrews 9:27; Revelation 21:4

DIFFICULTIES (Discipline through)

Romans 8:28; Hebrews 5:8; Hebrews 12:7; 2 Timothy 4.7, 8 ; Hebrews 12:5 ; Revelation 3:19

DISAPPOINTMENT

Psalms 43:5; Psalms 55:20; Psalms 126:6; II Corinthians 4:8, 9 ; John 14:27

FEAR

Psalms 27:1 Psalms 56:11; Proverbs 3.25; Isaiah 51:12; John 14:27; Romans 8:31 ; II Timothy 1:7; 1 John 4:18.

FORGIVENESS OF SIN

Psalms 32:5 ; Psalms 51 ; Psalms 103:3 ; Proverbs 28:13 ; Isaiah 1:18 ; Isaiah 55: 71; John 1:9 ; James 5:15, 16.

FORGIVING OTHERS

Matthew 5:44-47; Matthew 6:12; Matthew 6:14; Mark 11:25; Ephesians 4:32; Colossians 3:13.

GROWING SPRITUALLY

Ephesians 3:17-19; Colossians 1:9-11; Timothy 4:15 ; II Timothy 2.15 ; I Peter 2:2 ; Il Peter 1:5-8 ; Il Peter 3:18.

GUIDANCE

Psalms 32:8; Isaiah 30:21; Isaiah 58:11 ; John 16:13

HELP AND CARE

II Chronicles 16:9

BIBLIOGRAPHY

Adams JAY, *Competent to Counsel: Introduction to Nouthetic Counselling*, Grand Rapids, Zondervan Publishing House, 1986, 320 p.

Adams JAY, *The Christian Counselor's Manual: The Practice of Nouthetic Counselling*, Grand Rapids, Zondervan Publishing House,1986, 496 p.

Andrea ROUSE, *Christian counselling* (Doctorate dissertation), Canadian Christian Theological Seminary, 2013.

Angelo BRUSCO, *Counselling pastoral et Counselling psychologique: similitudes et différences*, (Master Essai), Ulaval, 1983.

Alain DENEUX, François-Xavier POUDAT, Thierry SERVILLAT, Jean-Luc VENISSE, *Les psychothérapies: approche plurielle*, Masson, 2009,464 p.

Brian SCHWERTLEY, "Biblical Principles for Solving Problems in the Home", Lansing, Michigan, 1996, 14 p.

Carole GREENWALD, Joanne Greer, Kevin Gillespie, Thomas Greer "A Study of the Identity of Pastoral Counselors", *American Journal of Pastoral Counselling*, 7:4, (2014), p.51-69.

Carl ROGERS, *Le développement de la personne*, Paris, Dunod-InterÉdition, 2005.

Carl ROGERS, ''Les caractéristiques d'une approche centrée sur la personne'', *ACP Pratique et recherche*, http://www.acp-pr.org/caracteristiques.html. visited on 2017-04-30.

Claire SQUIRES, Pierre JOUANNET, Jean-Philippe WOLF, Dominique CABROT, Jean-Marie KUNTSMANN. *Psychopathologie et procréation médicalement assistée : Comment les couples infertiles élaborent-ils la demande d'enfant?* Devenir, 2008 (2) Vol. 20, pages 135-149.

Christyne BONNEAU, *Approches systémiques et Thérapeutique familiale* (Master's thesis), Université Laval, 1991.

Christyne BONNEAU, *Le cadre thérapeutique selon diverses approches en psychothérapie* (Master's thesis), 1991, Université Laval.

Clinebell, J. HOWARD, *Basic Types of Pastoral Care & Counselling : Mariage Enrichment and Mariage Crisis Counselling*, Ressources for the Ministry of Healing and Growth, Nashville, Abingdon Press, 1984, pp. 243-282.

Clyde NARRAMORE, *Psychology of Counselling*, Grand Rapids, Michigan, Zondervan Publishing House, 1960, 304 p.

David A. POWLISON, *Seeing with New Eyes*, Phillipsburg, N.J., P & R Publishing Company, 2003, 274 p.

David A. POWLISON, ''*Counselling is the Church*'', *The Journal of Biblical Counselling*, 2015, p. 43-5.

David L. LUECKE, '' *Counselling with Couples.* '' *Pastoral Counselling.* New Jersey, Prentice-Hall, Inc., 1983, p.178-200.

Daniel W. HALE, Harold G. KOENIG, *Healing Bodies and Souls : A Pratical Guide for Congregations, Caring for Body, Mind, and Spirit,* Minneapolis, Fortress Press, 2003, p. 81-92.

Deana ADAMS, *Counselling and Spiritual Formation, Journal of Religion, Spirituality & Aging*, 21, 2009, p.131–141.

Donald, GUTHRIE, *Nouveau commentaire biblique*, Saint-Legier, Edition Emmaüs, 1978.

Ed WELCH, *What Is Biblical Counselling, Anyway? The Journal of Biblical Counselling*, Vol. 16, N. 1, 1997, p 1-5.

Élise BOUDREAULT, *Le cadre thérapeutique selon diverses approches en psychothérapie*, (Master thesis), ULaval, 1998.

Esther E. ACOLTSE, "Christian divorce Counselling in west Africa: Seeking Wholeness Through Reformed Theology and Jungian Dreamwork", *Journal of Pastoral Theology*, 21:1,2011, p. 2-1-2-18,

Emmanuel Y. LARTEY," *Pastoral Counselling in Multi-Cultural Contexts*," *International Perspectives on Pastoral Counselling*. The Haworth Press, Inc. 2000, p. 317-329.

Florent, VARAK, "L'Esprit dans la vie chrétienne". *La revue de théologie de la Faculté Jean Calvin*. Articles du n°260. Sommaire N° 260-mai 2011-nov. 2011-Tome LXII.

Fred C. GINGRICH, James Reaves FARRIS, " Pastoral Counselling in the Philippines", International Perspectives on Pastoral Counselling. The Haworth Press, Inc. 2000, p. 5-55.

George NEDUMARUTHUMCHALIL, " *The role of religion and spirituality in marriage and family therapy*", Journal of Pastoral Counselling; Vol. 44,2009, p.14-19.

Hubert W. Stroup, & Norma Schweitzer Wood, *Sexuality and the Counselling Pastor : The Tradition and Pastoral Counselling in Sexuality*. Philadelphia, Fortress Press, 1974, p.13-33.

J. Mark KILLMER, "The Treatment of Anxiety Disorders in Devout Christian Clients", *Journal of Family Psychotherapy*, 13:3-4, 2002, p.309-327.

Jean BERGERET, *La cure psychanalytique sur divan : les grandes découvertes sur la psychanalyse*, Tchou, 1980, p. 9-19.

Jean-Marie AUWERS, "La nuit de Nicodème" (Jn 3 :2 ; 19 :39) ou l'ombre du langage", *Revue biblique*, 1990, p. 481-503.

Jenkins TERRANCE, *Christian Counselling: Godly Principles to Help You in Time of Need*. Baltimore, Publish America, 2009, 83 p.

Jenkins TERRANCE, *Free Indeed: How to be free from demonic influence and addictive behaviors*, Baltimore, Publish America, 2006, 117p.

John FOSKETT, "Pastoral Counselling", British Journal of Guidance and Counselling Volume 23 No. 1, January 1985, p. 98-111.

I. S. W. I. T., "Mariage" *Le Grand Dictionnaire de la Bible*, Cléon d'Andran, Excelsis, 2014, p. 1007-1011.

John MACARTHUR, *La Sainte Bible avec commentaires de John MacArthur*, Genève, Société Biblique de Genève, 1979, 1582 p

John R. COMPTON, *"Premarital Preparation and Counselling"* Pastoral Counselling. New Jersey, Prentice-Hall, Inc., 1983, p.153-177.

Kirsty Rowan and Karen Dwyer, *"Demonic possession and deliverance in the diaspora: phenomenological descriptions from Pentecostal deliverees"* Journal of Mental Health, Religion & Culture, Vol. 18 (6), 2015, p. 440-455.

Louise M. MEEKS, James Reaves FARRIS, *"Global Issues of Pastoral Counselling: With Particular Attention to the Issues of Pastoral Counselling in the Philippines"*. *International Perspectives on Pastoral Counselling*, The Haworth Press, Inc. 2000, p. 57-75.

Margrit EICHLER, "Mariage au Canada" Encyclopédie canadienne, septembre 2016.

Matthew S. STANFORD, Demon or disorder: A survey of attitudes toward mental illness in the Christian church. Journal of Mental Health, Religion & Culture, Vol. 10 (5), 2007, p. 445-449.

N. SINELNIKOFF, *Les psychothérapies: inventaire critique.* Paris, ESF éditeur, 1993

Natasha Petty LEVERT (2007), *A Comparison of Christian and Non-Christian Males, Authoritarianism, and Their Relationship to Internet Pornography Addiction / Compulsion,* Sexual Addiction & Compulsivity, 14:2, p.145-166.

Newman S. CRYER Jr., John Monroe VAYHINGER, *Casebook in pastoral counselling,* New York, Abingdon Press, 1962, p. 20-31; 76-113.

Paul David TRIPP, Instruments dans les mains du Rédempteur, Montréal, Éditions Cruciforme, 2013, 504 p. (Traduit de l'édition originale en anglais: Instruments in the Redeemer's Hands, 2002)

Paul HOFF, *Le pasteur et la Cure d'âme : Mariage, Sexualité et Fiançailles.* Miami, Éditions VIDA, 1986, p. 77-86.

Paul HOFF, *Le pasteur et la Cure d'âme : Facteur conduisant à l'harmonie conjugale.* Miami, Editions VIDA, 1986, p. 87-.102.

Paul HOFF, *Le pasteur et la Cure d'âme : Cure d'âme avant et pendant le mariage ; la séparation.* Miami, Éditions VIDA, 1986, p. 102-115.

Paul HOFF, *Le pasteur et la Cure d'âme : Problèmes sexuels,* Miami, Éditions VIDA, 1986, p. 117-130.

Paul HOFF, *Le pasteur et la Cure d'âme : Le contrôle des émotions,* Miami, Editions VIDA, 1986, p. 188-203.

Paul HOFF, *Le pasteur et la Cure d'âme : La dépression et le suicide*, Miami, Éditions VIDA, 1986, p. 205-217.

Paul MILLEMAN, *La relation d'aide, vocation de l'Église*. France, Éditions Excelsis, 2014. 480 p.

Peter M. GUBI "A Qualitative Exploration of the Similarities and Differences between Counselling and Spiritual Accompaniment", Practical Theology, 4:3, 2011, p. 339-358.

Peter M. GUBI, *"An exploration of the use of Christian prayer in mainstream counselling"*, British Journal of Guidance & Counselling, 29:4, 2001, p.425-434,

Richard W. ROUKEMA, *Counselling for the* Soul in Distress : Counselling for the Soul in Distress: What Every Religious Counselor Should about Emotional and Mental Illness, New-York, Harworth, 2003, p.31-82

Simon YIU, Chuen LEE, *"Pastoral Counselling in Chinese Culture Contexts: Philosophical, Historical, Sociological, Spiritual and Psychological Considerations". International Perspectives on Pastoral Counselling*, The Haworth Press, Inc. 2000, p. 119-149.

Sodi et al., *Marriage and Counselling in African Communities: Challenges and Counselling Approaches, Journal of Psychology in Africa, 20(2),2010, p. 335–340.*

Sonia GREENIDGEA, Martyn BAKERB, *Why do committed Christian clients seek counselling with Christian therapists ? Counselling Psychology Quarterly*, Vol. 25, No. 3, September 2012, p. 211–222.

Sylva DENNIS, "Nicodemus and his Spices (Jn 19. 39)", New Testament Studies, 34, 1988, p.148-151.

Wayne GRUDEN, *Théologie systématique*, Éditions Excelsis, 2010, p.699.

William KIRWAN, ''*Biblical Concepts for Christian Counselling, A case for Integrating Psychology and Theology*'', Baker Book House Company, Grand Rapids, 1984.

Www.doctissimo.fr/grossesse/infertilite/causes-de-l-infertilite/infertilite-psychologique#qu-est-ce-que-l-infertilite-psychologique-nbsp.Website consulted on 26-03-2019

Www.encyclopediecanadienne.ca/fr/article/mariage-et-divorce/.Website consulted on 2017-06-05